WHAT NOBODY TOLD ME

An Entrepreneur's Journey

You can bring your dream to reality.

Augustina Hinds

ccp

March, 2023

Caribbean Chapters Publishing

ISBN (paperback): 979-8857-774-50-2

Dedicated to my dear clients for being part of my journey.

Table of Contents

Acknowledgements

My deepest thanks to the Supreme Creator for Divine guidance.

I salute those people who were there for me during this journey. All that they offered was well appreciated. Countless teachers have come into my life. I let their teachings carry me to greater heights and understanding.

Thanks to all those who helped keep the restaurant doors open. Much gratitude to my faithful clients. You have become valued friends.

I express sincere thanks to Terry Haynes who took that bold step and started the business with me. I was fortunate to have his phenomenal support and many contributions along the way.

Ian Estwick deserves special mention for his invaluable backing at the inception of the restaurant. It was a wonderful blessing. Thank you profoundly.

I am tremendously grateful to my editor Carol Pitt for helping to make this book what it is. I admire her professionalism and the meticulous way she approaches the editing process. You are great to work with.

I would like to acknowledge Suresh Chatrani who usually appears at the right time. He rescued me when I was having technical problems with my laptop. Thank you.

Many thanks are due to Junior Allsopp for the business and personal favours I have received in this journey. Your kindness will forever be remembered.

I am really appreciative of the assistance Andrew Connell, Peter Mayers, Victor Bishop, and Charles Lowe have offered me. I can always call on them, even at the last hour. Thanks guys.

A special thank you to Wilma Halloway who brought her wisdom to our conversations.

I want to thank Stanton Elcock, my former schoolmate. He is also an entrepreneur, and our chats were illuminating and filled with lots of laughter which was good for me while writing this book.

During lunch time my phone would ring just a few minutes after 1 o'clock, and I knew it was Roger Moore on the other end. He would say: "I am on my way." I want to especially thank him for his immense support over several years at the restaurant.

Arturo Tappin, Ian Durant, Shelley Carrington, Noel Burke, Lionel Weekes and Denis McIntosh, I am grateful to you all for your extraordinary contributions.

Ayanna Young, thanks for your helpful suggestions and being part of my journey.

I am thankful to Vonda Smith for her loving, caring and sharing nature and to Clairmonte Blanche for his encouragement. You both made a world of difference.

Thanks to Charles Lewis for the many inspirational quotes you send me daily; they urged me on as I wrote this book.

Timing is everything. Uncle Kelvin, thanks for showing up. I truly enjoy your presence.

Much gratitude to my dear sister Maymona for her thoughtfulness and generosity.

Most of all, my wholehearted thanks to my children Jamila, Sade and Shomari who stood with me throughout the business years.

Introduction

I have been a restaurateur for over 25 years. I have chosen to share my journey so that it might benefit new entrepreneurs who are at the beginning of theirs. I also want to encourage individuals who are bold to take that first step towards their dream.

People often say they will take action "when the right time comes". The right time is now. Just start. To those people who have brilliant ideas, implement them. To those already in business, I congratulate you for your bravery.

Let me say to that person who has a special talent that it is your gift and you can use it. You have a skill that comes naturally to you; and you know what you are good at. What is your talent? What do you have a knack for? At a time when entrepreneurship is more widespread you can turn your hobby into a full-time business.

Even though this book is about business, many of the principles mentioned can apply to life in general. With this book I aim to offer some form of mental stimulation to the reader. I can only share my own experience. I write like this because I have lived it and I want to show that anything is possible. Trust yourself; that's what matters.

May this narrative inspire those who are dealing with a challenge or contemplating a life change. It is my intention that my writing will be useful to people from almost every walk of life.

The Journey is the Goal

I always knew I wanted my own business. The idea would not go away. To start a business from scratch and watch it grow is a wonderful feeling. The experience is beyond all I could ever imagine. It is vast! The joy of being able to give a part of myself to make a difference through my work is fulfilling.

I have about three decades in the culinary industry under my belt. How did I reach this far? I love what I do. Love is key to survival. Love held everything together. Love was the glue. I committed myself wholeheartedly to the business. I stuck with it 'through thick and thin', making it the finest it could be.

There is gratification in creating a product and putting it on the market. The journey can be overwhelming at times, but there is comfort in finding true purpose here on planet earth. It is difficult to walk away from something you are passionate about. Passion is the fuel that feeds the hunger and thirst of the vision.

Sometimes fatigue sets in and I ask myself: "What

am I doing?" But if not me, then who? I quote Rumi as saying "It's your road, and yours alone. Others may walk it with you but no one can walk it for you."

At night I lay in bed and give thanks for being able to complete the day's activities. There is a sense of satisfaction. I rejoice at the slightest accomplishment, and the next morning I start all over again. I know the work 'by heart'; the ins and outs and the quicker ways to get it done. It's like second nature. Competence has come with the years. It is a by-product of diligent work. The task gets easier with practice and you become more efficient. Less effort is required; you just flow.

Pursue that 'calling' you carry deep in your heart and put it into something definite. Listen to the whispers. In spite of the pitfalls you may encounter along the way, make it happen. I found that pitfalls would somehow give me a little nudge to be my authentic self.

You have the ability to achieve your dream, whether it is education, a profession, music, sports, the arts or business. Whatever you choose, do it with the greatest love.

The art of taking the risk

I had limited cash, but I had no fear. I had a true sense of purpose. Somehow I knew that extra funds would come from somewhere. Infinite intelligence guided me and I started to prepare for the restaurant. I applied for a bank loan. I went shopping for some essential equipment as though I had already obtained the loan. Trust gives so much power. And then it happened, the loan was approved. This money helped to purchase other major supplies for the business, bringing everything together. I guess the bank's loan officer liked the idea and had some measure of confidence in what was presented in the business plan.

Are you a risk taker? Are you ready to take the risk?

Taking risks is about that yearning you have for attainment, not only for financial gains, but also for your personal satisfaction. It has to do with self-concept—the worthiness you hold for yourself. You know what you want, and why you want it.

To have your own business involves some measure of risk taking. You have to make up your mind that you can stick it out. The staying power is solely yours. It is up to you. All I am offering here is the truth, nothing more.

Business is a game, especially when it's your own. You take a chance and no matter the constraints you are driven, as the need to succeed is great. Play the cards you are dealt. Winning has to do with how you play them. Every now and then the stakes are heavy, but study your hand carefully. Sometimes you may need to reshuffle the cards in order to win. Who likes losing? There is joy in winning.

The restaurant business is unpredictable, yet I take that chance every day. Unless you have pre-orders or a catering contract for special occasions, there is no guarantee who is going to show up. It is a gamble. Some days are busy with customers while other days are moderate or slow. At times the risk can be too much. On those days I ask myself why I thought it was okay to get into the industry. However, I shrug off that feeling and simply continue. I live with each day as it comes. I take the bitter with the sweet and make it work. Although it is risky, I manage somehow and for me that is the thrill.

I have been through tough moments, but they pass. When business is slow, reevaluate your methods to make it better. Be bold and do something out of the ordinary to boost sales and to meet your needs. Put your heart into it until you reach your demand. That period of slowness helps you uncover another side of you. It awakens the genius in you.

The restaurant business is tangible and intangible. Many underlying factors are involved and you are constantly asking yourself questions. Is this the right move? Should I take more risk? Can I sustain it by just breaking even? (Note that to break-even is to make neither a loss nor profit.) Only you can access the progress. Trust yourself to walk its unpredictable course and stay on track because you never know where it will lead you. Be willing to take the risk. Rewards come from taking risks.

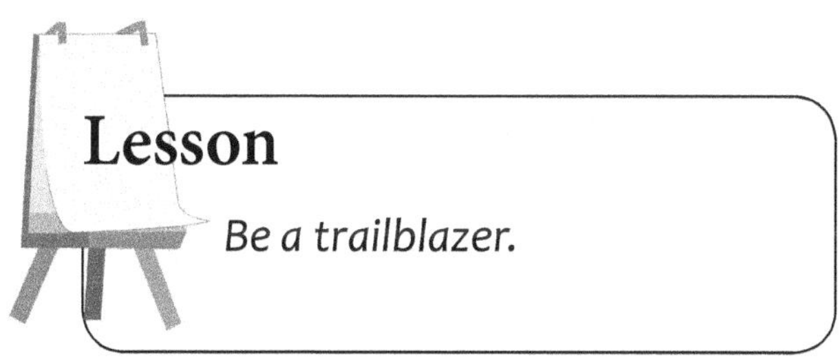

Lesson

Be a trailblazer.

Hit or miss in business

I am elated with the hits, but what about the misses? Rather than fret over the misses I had to make sense of what was going on. I revised my strategy and adjusted here and there to find a way out. As you manoeuvre you get better and in the end you become adept at getting it right. The misses can often be our greatest teachers.

You can enhance what already exists by bringing extra flair to the presentation. You don't have to create something new. Sometimes it is better to stick with the tried and tested product to maintain the clientele you would have built up over the years. 'A bird in the hand is worth two in the bush', especially in these times of extreme uncertainty. That strong client base is what usually keeps the business in a stable position.

In addition, you might have to diversify. Whether it is enhancement of the product or diversification, select what is more suitable for you. Another path for the business might call for you to revamp the product. In the grand scheme of things, do what you are comfortable with and continue to nurture your dream. We all have that desire to succeed.

Gains and losses

In business there are gains and losses. Are you ever totally prepared for a loss? What is your next step? Are you going to stay and manage? You must be decisive. It is wise to evaluate and reexamine your situation first. Be practical in your approach and look at the available choices. Let your choices cultivate growth.

In my experience, the loss was part of the learning process. I looked at life from both sides and got on with my dream. I valued what was left and made it work for me. I found something in each day to celebrate. Don't lament over the losses, for you have the capability to rise above them. There is so much within you just waiting to emerge. The gift is ready to work for you. Utilize your creative power. You never know how much you can do until you do it. You have the freedom to act.

Tell yourself: "I am doing a good job". Work with what remains and do not upset yourself with what you have lost. There is so much more to life.

Now let us look at the gain. See the intrinsic value of your achievement and celebrate it. Recognize the good fortune you possess. You earned it. Put aside money when business is doing well. You might start out with one goal and then branch out into other things. Decide whether you want to continue with the same or develop a new project. Decide if you want to expand. Nevertheless, with the rising cost of raw materials for production, you should tread carefully. Don't be complacent; monitor your activities so that you can sustain a manageable price which can benefit you as well as your client. The gain is also a great teacher.

Lessons in business

In business, lessons are always being taught and it is up to you to comprehend the message. Messages comes in various ways. Open your eyes and ears to receive them. Let wisdom prevail as you interpret the deeper meaning. Most things we encounter usually serve their purpose, whether it is in business or our personal life. We may not understand them when they are happening at that particular time, but in due course we recognize the things life has brought and taught us.

A door may be closed in your face, but in business you can't take it personally. It is best left alone. Continue your journey knowing that as you knock, other doors of opportunity will open for you; that as you ask more than enough is given; that as you seek the most amazing things you find. Do what's in your heart. Do what you do with excellence and feel great about your deeds.

Was it really a surprise or did you see it coming a long time ago? There are adverse consequences when we ignore an imbalance. Address an issue as it emerges. Nip it in the bud early. Decide to act. Don't procrastinate. Is there something you do not approve of? Then handle it forthwith.

You must pay attention to the smallest detail. It is usually there staring you in the face. Watch the pattern. The pattern is often seasonal. Before I come to a conclusion, I examine carefully first. I often look at every detail and at the full picture. Before you conclude, consider. Do not be too hasty. Weigh the pros and cons. Sometimes the final decision has to do with how urgent it is.

You are on course, but an unfortunate situation develops. What should you do? First, keep your composure. It helps you to function in the difficulty. Second, maintain a flexible attitude. It gives you the ability to adapt irrespective of what is taking place. Third, sometimes you have to accept and empty yourself. When we accept, it brings peace of mind. See the silver lining in the situation. It can be a blessing in disguise. Things happen to us, but they can lead us to a better way of life.

There is a lot to learn from business. Each day has its moments, and the journey continues. It becomes an adventure which makes the whole process more fascinating. Skip along merrily and enjoy each step of the journey. Some days you travel along beautiful terrain, other days you have to pick your way around rough patches and uneven tracks. At times you edge your way carefully through the narrow paths. Listen to your heart.

Lesson

Even in setbacks there are positive aspects. Keep going after your dream. Interruptions require swift action.

Living the Dream

Be unstoppable

Life, with its unforeseeable behaviour, can take you to a place you would hardly ever have envisioned. After much effort towards keeping the business alive, the big blow came that wanted to topple years of devoted work. I was aware of the fact that life gives tests and this was just another. I was being taught in the most powerful way. I was in a let-go situation. I was in transition, and I flowed with it. My response to everything was to be grateful for each day of life.

I began each morning saying: "Today is a great day" and finished the evening saying: "Today is a great day". I didn't know where all this was taking me, but I felt that some good would evolve from it. I was adamant that I would not let myself down. It involved a lot of mental conditioning. I convinced myself that it would be alright. The positive attitude helped.

Finally things started to improve, and this was an encouraging sign. I promised myself never to give up until I arrived at the ultimate goal. I kept true to my cause. The drawback allowed me to fully recognize my potential, to decide what I definitely wanted to do, and to express who I really am.

Are you ever prepared for that big blow when it strikes? Probably not, but you must hold firm. Sometimes things happen for your greater good. Be disciplined to walk your unique path. You have to stay strong. No one can be strong for you, so be strong for yourself. I call it self-preservation. You have enough of your own strength to carry you through. Go within and put resources to use. Know that life has its surprises, but you cannot give up on yourself. Life is waiting on you to rescue you. Follow your guiding star.

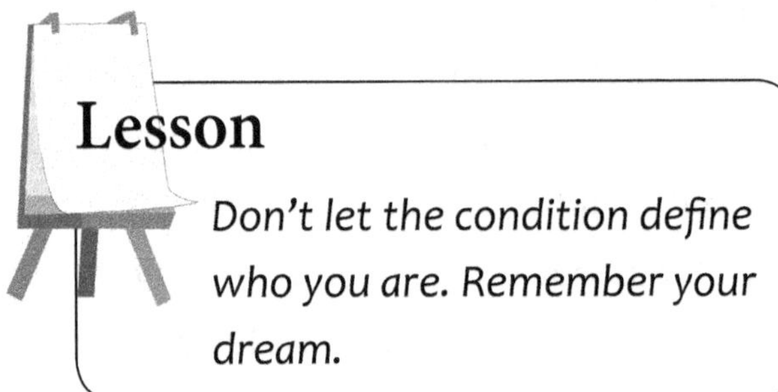

Lesson

Don't let the condition define who you are. Remember your dream.

Be unattached to expectations

We don't get everything we ever wanted. When your expectations are not fulfilled, do not grieve.

Instead, continue to pursue your endeavour. Remember that not getting what you want is sometimes an extraordinary stroke of luck.

When things don't go according to your expectations you have to let go of the life you planned. Letting go doesn't mean that you are giving up, but that you are taking a different path.

Sometimes you have to step back and look closer at the event to see where it wants to take you. Sometimes doing nothing works to your advantage. It allows you the 'caterpillar' to change into a 'butterfly'.

The power of resilience

The sign said 'men at work'. There was lots of drilling and dust everywhere. The road in front of the restaurant was under massive construction and therefore disrupted the usual flow of traffic. People were avoiding the area and those who dared to come had to proceed with much caution. I was hardly seeing customers and I was grateful for the few regulars that trickled in. The reduction in sales definitely had an effect on the business. The rent was long overdue. Utility bills were to be paid, but I still smiled. It cost me nothing to smile.

The customers saw that smile, braveness and

cool demeanor but could never imagine what was happening underneath it. I shed secret tears for myself and the business. The tears were my prayers. I can remember quite vividly that the repairs seemed to be taking ages to finish. I had to gather much grit to be able to keep functioning.

During the day I was thinking about the business. At night I was thinking about the business. I fell asleep thinking about the business. As I slept I dreamt about the business. I woke up thinking about the business. It felt like every breath involved thinking about what to do next. I had to stop over-thinking, so I shifted my thoughts. I formed a picture in my mind and visualized a booming, prosperous business.

The quiet inner voice of courage urged me on every day. There was no turning back. I knew my intention for the restaurant, so I acknowledged all that was going on and rode it out. I did my conceivable best to make things happen; to make the restaurant thrive. I realized that keeping it simple helped to lessen the complications I had at hand.

I dealt with the most pressing issue I faced daily. I held on until the road was completed and things returned to normal once again. Things got better and I got rid of my debts. Overcoming the financial dilemma was a tremendous relief.

In the deep waters you have to outsmart the sharks to avoid being eaten alive. From out of the deep waters I moved forward with confidence to solid ground. To move forward with boldness is to be truly empowered. When you are empowered you have such vibrant energy and this is what sustains the dream. I knew I could make it.

What did I learn from the whole episode? Not to stress myself out with what is beyond my control. Do not give power to the condition. Sleep peacefully.

Why complain about external circumstances? Accept the things you cannot change and have the courage to change the things you can. The key is to make the most out of every day. Trust that everything will work out favourably. Do not hold a scarcity mindset. Sow thoughts of abundance and success. Call your desires into being.

What was I preparing for? Probably there was a lesson I needed to learn. As time went on I became aware of what I was being prepared for. The experience molded me for other challenges later in life. The experience proved to be useful in many ways. It was good preparation moving forward. It has certainly taught me to get along with little, to be versatile, and to bounce back quickly.

Each day I wake up and say "I can do this. It is possible." Then I continue bravely into the unknown.

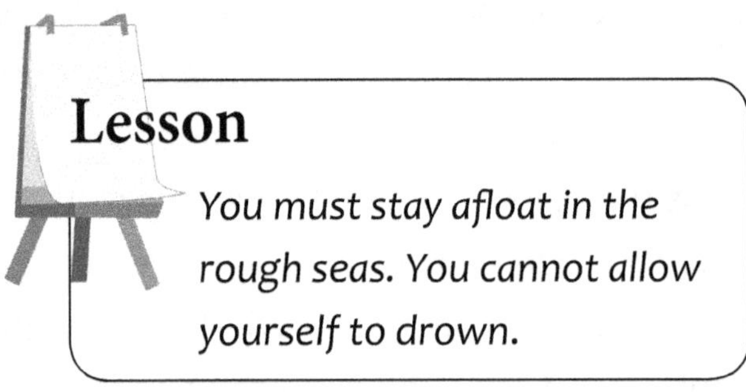

Handling disruptions

It is amazing how life changes at any given time. It was the year 2020. The global Covid-19 pandemic came and brought with it many interruptions. Strict protocols were put in place and we could not operate as usual. There were also the lockdowns and the curfews which restricted levels of movement. I had to face them all and deal with the situation as I saw fit.

During the lockdowns I made wise use of my time. I kept busy being productive. I got my hands into the dirt and I planted vegetables and herbs in my backyard garden. I also spruced up the flower beds. The gardening was the perfect form of exercise. It felt good being outside. It brightened my Spirit. I had ample time to catch up on things I kept putting off and I did some necessary improvements to the house.

The kitchen became a 'lab' and I experimented with my culinary ideas. I prepared a variety of delightful vegan dishes. I enjoy the art of food plating, so I practiced arranging food to create attractive and colourful presentations. I also concentrated on writing, and I was able to produce the book *You Can Breathe*. There was no rush and I could explore my thoughts.

Things were happening quickly and before you got a grip on one situation, another was at your door step. In my country, Barbados, we endured the volcanic ash from an eruption in a nearby island, which was a major setback. This was followed by a storm which added to the chaos. Everything was having a ripple effect on general living and on the economy. We were all in this together. Everyone was affected. We were all coping and getting along in different ways.

I kept adapting and faring with each circumstance I encountered. Restaurants were closed for a considerable time. I have been in other dire situations and I was totally prepared for this one. I responded to the closure with an open mind and was able to find a way around it. 'Waste not, want not' was my motto. I re-used, reduced, recycled, repurposed and repaired whenever possible. These basic techniques were workable and helped me in my daily living. I accomplished much with what I had. Being super-thrifty eased the pressure. I defied all the odds I was up against and became aware of what I could pull off. I kept the dream alive, not by backing down from the challenges, but by facing them head on.

In times like these I would suggest that you resort to the thing you know. It works. Pour your energies into it. Develop resourceful habits and behaviour. In some areas you might have to improvise and make do with what is conveniently on hand. It is worth mentioning that with less I became more creative with what I had available. Human beings possess a built-in mechanism which gets us through. We have the ability to develop strategies, and to construct ways to see ourselves out of our predicaments.

There was something mystical about all the happenings. What would we discover through all this? What was it telling us? I am of the opinion that these disruptions were more likely leading us to truly look at ourselves; to have a mindful approach to life; to look for alternative methods to get things done; to become more innovative; to explore new horizons; to shift our mindsets. Every phase in our lives teaches us something valuable.

When I analyzed the whole episode I came to the conclusion that life was taking me in another direction. Change can be scary, but I embraced the change, and by changing I experienced inner growth. Don't resist the change. It could be simply a turning point in your life. Be open to it. Recognize that change is also an opportunity for advancement. Know that change takes courage. Change for the better. Be the change that you want to see. Change sometimes leads us in the direction of our destiny.

What did I learn during the disruptions? I learned to value what's important in my life. One thing the global pandemic has taught me is to do all the things I envision. Just create and live the life I want.

Be prepared for anything. Do not let the strain cause you to lie down. It is not necessary to strain yourself. Go within and feel alright. The wisdom you now possess is much greater than what you would have begun with, thus allowing you to manage whatever may come your way. You have a lot to smile about; a smile which says 'I have conquered and overcome once again.'

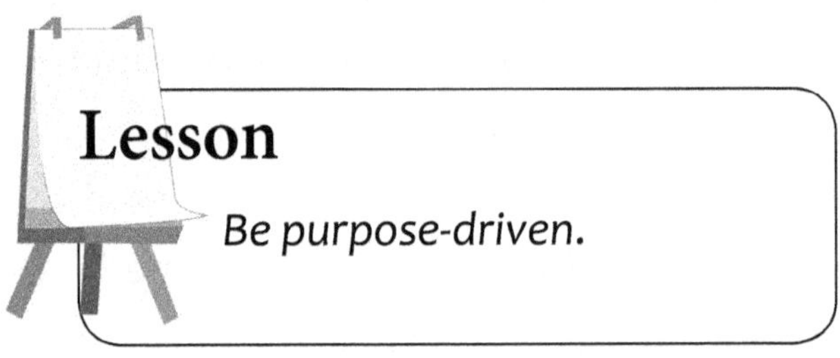

In retrospect re-examination

People usually say that we should refrain from revisiting the past, but sometimes the memories allow us to connect the dots. I found that looking back showed me what not to repeat. It was about being reflective on how I overcame and not that I was reliving some undesirable issue. It was more or less retrieving the techniques that were helpful. I took the best from the past. You can find solutions by drawing from your previous experiences.

I would have confronted some hiccups, but they prepared me well going forward. I can see the good purpose for all of them. I learnt what not to do and what to do. I have much better knowledge than when I first started on this journey.

Your past gives you the wisdom you possess. Now you know how to prepare. You are not starting from square one; you have a head start. You are starting from experience. What you learn never leaves you.

When I reflected on my business career, my greatest discoveries were in the challenges. I realized that when I was going through challenges I grew the most. I have found that the challenges inspired my creativity. The more I create, the more joyful I am.

Everything had meaning and was for a purpose. Victories, problems, obstacles and adversity, wins, gains, losses, challenges—I can go on and on—are all my valuable teachings.

Can you be victorious even in defeat? I must say yes. The wondrous teaching of defeat was a fortunate occurrence and added to my life. It helped me to grow. Now I use the word 'opportunity' more often in my vocabulary and language instead of dwelling on negativity.

The waiting

I wait. The wait seems long most of the time, yet I wait. *For what?* I often ask myself, although I already know. The short answer is to see where everything leads me. I have so many ideas of what I want to accomplish on this journey that the wait is worth it. Sometimes I was restless; still I waited. I am only a player in the game. During the wait I became more aware that all things are possible.

Many people give up just before the breakthrough. Sometimes we spend our time being anxious, but do not be fixated about the outcome. Instead, grind it out until it becomes actual. Be full of excitement while waiting for the result. Wait with a song in your heart. Simply wait. It comes. It's like a pregnant woman waiting with her first child. There is often joy in the surprise.

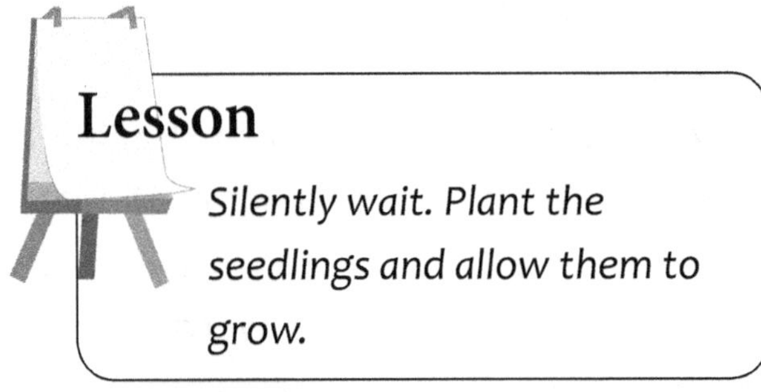

Lesson

Silently wait. Plant the seedlings and allow them to grow.

What have I learnt?

I learnt that dreams become reality. You must do the leg work and have trust in your own power to make it happen. Each day you do your utmost until you prosper. Know that you are contributing to this world by providing a service that is needed. You can make your dreams a reality.

It is about bravery. Be brave enough to push forward despite the challenges and changes. Go beyond your situation. An opportunity might come in a disguised form. Don't let its appearance fool you. Don't judge the book by its cover.

I have learnt to keep expenses as low as possible in order to meet financial obligations for the business and personal affairs.

I have learnt that two people can look at the same thing and see it differently. It is all about perception. Some significant things business life has taught me are: not to let go of my values; not to settle for anything below my standard; to never lose my identity; and to hold on to my integrity.

Keep people around who add to your life; you need positive vibration. Keep people in your life that actually love you, motivate you, encourage you, inspire you, enhance you, and that you are glad to be with. It is good to have someone that shines the light in your life.

Keep people around you who are trustworthy. Identify who values you. Know when you are valued and that what you have to say counts. Never feel undervalued.

I have learnt that problems can be outgrown and that knowledge is also gained by error, mess, or blunder. Everything can change in the blink of an eye. Whatever it is, trust that it will be fine. There is happiness when you embrace Self Worth. In times of confusion, focus on what you did right. Compliment yourself.

I have learnt not to anticipate, but to hold on with a heart full of love. I found myself no longer planning, and it feels good. Now I let go of fixed plans. I am not saying that you shouldn't plan, but detach yourself, otherwise the control can be too much.

Most of all I have learnt to be comfortable with who I am; to accept who I am; to live my life as I see fit; to live my purpose to the fullest. There is freedom in all of this.

Happy Memories: The Early Years

Errol Griffith (in the middle) who officially opened the restaurant on December 29th 1996 and some of his work colleagues.

Visitors to the island experiencing our lunch cuisine.

My niece Fountain and her family from Canada on vacation.

Me, Renette and David Berman with their two sons from Toronto.

The young and the elder: Wes Hall and my son Shomari eating together.

We catered for the Kelloggs Worthington Seminar at another venue.

Participants at the Kelloggs Seminar feasting on our vegan cuisine.

Me preparing a plate for a guest at this health-oriented event. Jenelle Layne, my workmate, also assisted with the serving.

Me taking time out to chat with Carol and Craig in December 1997.

Preparing the samples for a new line of Lomo Linda and Morning Star vegan products the agents were advertising.

Healthy lifestyle in the park where people are keen on getting information about wellness.

The Toppin family gathering was a great time.

Viola Toppin in red dress with family at her 90th birthday celebration.

My daughter Sade and I at the restaurant.

My daughter Jamila and I participated at a company's healthy lifestyle exhibition.

Fitzgerald Hinds from Trinidad with friends having lunch together.

This group took time off to have lunch together.

Marine biologist Andre Miller and Angie Brathwaithe took a break from the sea to have a bite and enjoy the ambience of the restaurant.

Junior Allsopp who was coming from inception of the restaurant.

Kelly-Ann, second from the left, with her mother and their friends at a special dinner night out.

Chanley and his work colleagues at lunch time.

These two tourists were very appreciative of the meal and service.

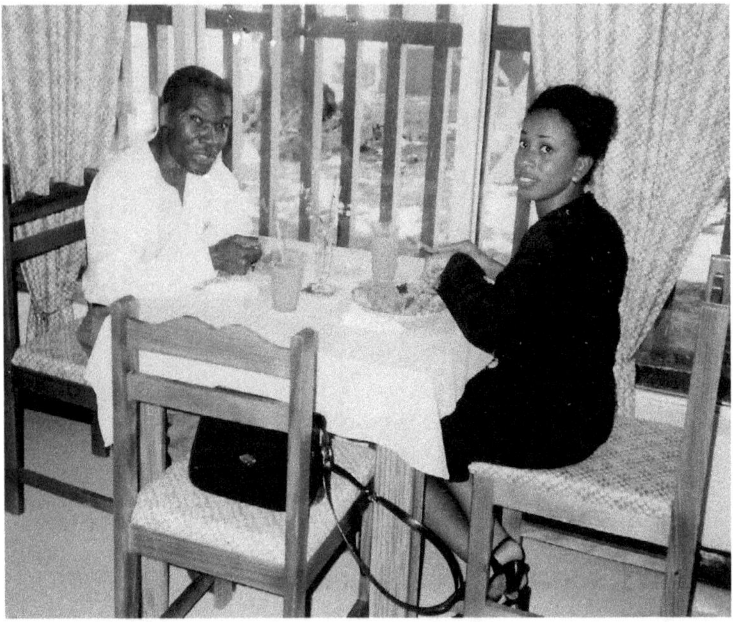

John Mwansa and his work colleague Paula having a relaxing time.

Professor Hilary Beckles and his work colleagues have much to smile about.

At the healthy lifestyle fairs in Queens Park many people usually came to our stall to see what we were offering and promoting.

Anthony 'Gabby' Carter and Eddie Grant with friends in the music industry.

FrontPage2
THE INSIDE COVER

TOAST TO TURO.

IT WAS HEALTHY EATING and a hearty celebration among good friends in the music fraternity yesterday, at a surprise celebration for internationally acclaimed saxophonist, Arturo Tappin who last week received one of Jamaica's top award – The Prime Minister's Award For Excellence.

At The Vegetarian, Black Rock, St Michael, Arturo was joined by his uncle, Elombe Mottley, cousin Stewart Mottley, Deepu Panjwani, Adrian "Boo" Husbands, Nicholas Brancker, AJA, Chris Harper, Chris Allman and Derek Walcott.

The celebration was organised by his mother, Dyne Mottley-Tappin and his brother Dai.

The Barbadian said he was surprised to be the only non-Jamaican of six music professionals to receive the prestigious award at the annual Jamaica Independence Gala last Saturday in Kingston.

"I did not know that I was receiving an award until I got there. From the moment we got to sound check I was just figuring out how to play with [The Riddim Twins] Lowell 'Sly' Dunbar and Robbie Shakespeare in the show," he said.

Tappin has been involved in the Jamaican music fraternity from the late 1980s, performing with reggae stars Mikey Bennett, surviving members of The Wailers, Dean Fraiser, Cedella Marley and Third World. He was first introduced by Sharon Burke, a promoter of the defunct Sun Splash reggae festival.

HERE'S TO YOU! The toast of the afternoon was Arturo Tappin (left). He was joined by (from left) cousin Stewart Mottley, Nicholas Brancker, Deepu Panjwani, uncle Elombe Mottley, Derek Walcott, Adrian "Boo" Husbands, Chris Harper, Chris Allman and AJA. (Picture by Sandy Pitt)

Arturo Tappin with fellow musicians and family members.

This family from England were among those who dined with us. The column next to them is adorned with photos of local and visitor patrons.

Vegetarian cuisine for healthy life style

NATION Editor Harold Hoyte and a business colleague enjoy The Vegetarian's lunchtime cuisine.

"The Vegetarian is a healthy way of life - not just eating.
"It is going to grow. It's in the air. I can feel it. It's birthing."
Restaurateur Augustina Hinds

The banker who turned down their loan application, questioning how many Barbadians were vegetarians, ought to (if only out of curiosity) stop in at The Vegetarian Restaurant at Block Rock, St. Michael, any day between 11 a.m. and 3 p.m.

Or, he may want to read some of the "thank you" letters by visitors from far away places, who not only enjoyed the all-vegetable cuisine but thought it was the highpoint of their stay in Barbados.

He could also check with hotel guests and determine the number of visitors who enquire about restaurants offering the cuisine found at The Vegetarian.

The pleasant, cosy restaurant, opened just more than 18 months ago in what was once the Block Rock branch office of the Royal Bank of Canada, has a growing lunchtime clientele that represents every class of the compartmentalised Barbadian society.

Academics, bankers, journalists and newspaper editors, entertainers of the elite order, artisans, visitors from Europe and North and South America; African, French, Spanish, Chinese and Indians - they all make The Vegetarian a social meeting place at lunch time.

Carol and Craig, apparently husband and wife visitors from California who experienced The Vegetarian last December 10 and 11, described it as the highlight of their visit to Barbados.

"So much for the delicious bread you gave us to take with us on the plane when we flew back to California the next day," they wrote in a January 1998 letter to restaurateur Augustina Hinds.

"Actually we ate it for breakfast while we were at the Barbados airport before our plane left.

"We appreciated your food and your hospitality and The Vegetarian was one of the highlights of our visit to Barbados," the two visitors wrote in their 'thank you' note.

Another visitor, Jane Palmer from England compared lunch at The Vegetarian to "an oasis" in the desert ... glorious and fulfilling".

Palmer told the restaurateur the roti she took for supper "was the best veggie pattie I've ever tasted. You must send me the recipe."

Augustina Hinds, a graduate of the Barbados Community College and the Barbados Institute of Management and Productivity (BIMAP), who has made food and nutrition her forte, says The Vegetarian "is a healthy way of life - not just eating".

"It is going to grow," she adds. "It's in the air. I can feel it. It's birthing."

Ms Hinds, who taught Food and Nutrition at a number of newer and older secondary schools, considered establishing her own business while studying Hotel Catering and Institutional Management at the Barbados Community College.

In addition to the BCC's two-year programme, she also studied Food Science Technology and complemented her Child Psychology training with a Management of Human Resources programme at BIMAP.

"It was a divine plan," she remarked, in her attempt to explain her preparation for the restaurant business.

"If you open something that is not the norm, people would want to see your credentials. It gives them more confidence," added Ms Hinds, who flaunts her BCC and BIMAP certificates on the restaurant walls, along with National Independence Festival of Creative Arts (NIFCA) awards that testify to her extraordinary, culinary skills.

Harold Hoyte and Lennox Prescod, a business colleague.

THE VEGETARIAN 10th Anniversary Special

Blessed with success

BUSINESSWOMAN **AUGUSTINE HINDS** believes the secret to her success over the last ten years could only be attributed to a covenant made with her Divine Maker.

Indeed, she makes it quite clear that if she were only in the restaurant business for the money, she would have quit long time ago.

Instead, she has been blessed with a gift of not only cooking well balanced, nutritious and creative vegetarian dishes, but being able to connect with all of her customers.

At The Vegetarian then, it is not merely an exchange of money for a meal as every customer leaves the restaurant fully contented.

Besides the serene ambience which immediately puts the customer at ease, patrons to the Black Rock, St Michael restaurant also seek and receive advice on the best way to prepare their own therapeutic vegetarian meals.

She also has a piece of advice to all those young aspiring entrepreneurs – no matter what field they have chosen.

"Keep focused, subscribe to relevant magazines and enrol in relevant courses to stay abreast with the changes in the business world," she said.

WHETHER THEY TAKE IT AWAY, or opt to have their meal in the "homey" atmosphere at The Vegetarian restaurant, customers are drawn to the tasty, therapeutic vegetarian meals served up by Augustine Hinds and her team.

THIS CUSTOMER is having his meal to go.

Newspaper feature on the restaurant as we celebrated our 10th anniversary.

Here I am with Nicole in the earlier times.

My friend Mandisa often frequented the restaurant on evenings.

Me, Terry Haynes, Andrea Wells and a judge at the Culinary Arts category during NIFCA, Oct. 2000.

Balancing Work and Personal Life

Healthy coping

Work can be stressful; life can be stressful. It is how you deal with the stress that makes the difference. You need to go with the flow. It releases the stress. Don't get overly concerned about trivial things. We get through them. Adhere to purposeful living.

Don't stress yourself out with what is not in your control. I started out not knowing how I would manage, yet at the end of the day most things were completed. I have learnt that it was not necessary to have put myself under pressure.

After a full day's work, I relinquish my mixed emotions over what I have been through. Then at night I drift off to sleep giving thanks for a fruitful day. Go to sleep feeling the success.

Have a sense of humor. Humor is good for the soul. Be jovial in your everyday life. It reduces your stress level.

Occasionally you don't feel like doing anything. Just stop even though you are eager about accomplishing your goal. It is okay to indulge in a little idleness. Shifting your thoughts to happy memories has a calming effect on the body.

Keep your life simple. When your life is simple it is less stressful. Contentment comes with simplicity. Contentment harbors joy and I can see how it relates to reaching every milestone in the business.

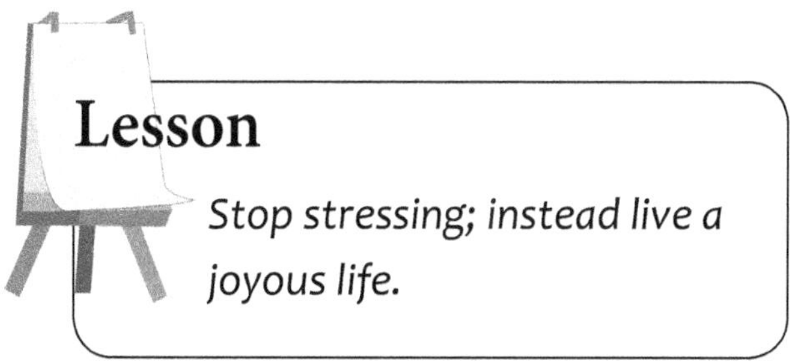

How to live with limited cash

I am telling it like it is, no pretending, no fancy frills and no polishing up.

Keep it real when there is scarcity of cash. Ask yourself "Do I really need this item? Is it affordable? Is it worth purchasing?" I am not suggesting that you shouldn't treat yourself, just reduce the level of unnecessary spending.

Be frugal in your business and personal life. You have to economize to get the benefit of the least. Manage what money you have by making careful choices. The less expensive product does not mean that it is inferior. Some low-priced goods are just as fine as the top brands. Just check the ingredients on their labels and you would realize they are exactly the same or comparable.

Be alert. Buy quality merchandise when it is marked down. Don't waste money on frivolous items when you have insufficient funds. Be discreet in the management of your money and resources.

To be able to stretch the monthly budget, look out for bargains. Shop at the flea market; you never know what you might find. Shop at the dollar store. It is amazing the stuff you can purchase there. Shop at the farmer's market; fruits and vegetables are much cheaper, especially when they are in season. Don't be afraid to ask for discounts. The sales attendant can either say 'yes' or 'no'.

Put aside some money. Save cash. You don't know what will happen. The world can be full of surprises. Every dollar counts. I store any loose change in a jar.

Know what things matter the most. Have a shopping list and stick to it. Don't overspend. When making purchases, I select quality over quantity.

Practice conscious spending. Know the value of your money. Did you get your money's worth? I stick with the grocery stores I know. Because I am a frequent shopper, the attendants have become familiar with me and look out for my best interests.

Avoid impulse buying. Don't be tempted to buy because the product is on sale. Keep and follow a budget. Monitor your cash flow. Know where every dollar goes. If you have the cash, avoid using credit.

Sometimes buying in bulk interferes with your cash reserves. Know your purchasing power and what you are capable of handling. It makes no sense using up your funds to get a few dollars off when that money can be evenly distributed to keep the business running. Nevertheless, I must say that if you can manage bulk buying then so be it. It has its advantages and can be convenient in some ways.

When cash is limited, stretch the dollar by purchasing a variety of items in smaller quantities. It make more sense, as it helps to keep the business running until more cash comes in. Today at the grocery stores you put whatever produce you want on the electronic scale and it gives you a price for that amount in weight. In my country, Barbados, there is an old saying: 'if you can't buy a pound, buy a half pound'.

Account for every dollar. I record whatever money comes in and goes out. I keep tabs on every single expense. When running a business you have to track your spending.

When it comes to organizing your finances, estimate, evaluate, record and tally are key words to have at your fingertips.

The truth, no sugar coating

There is this conceived notion about business: that it is a bed of roses. Let me dispel this common myth, as no one sees the behind-the-scenes of the entrepreneur. To be just plain and straightforward, sometimes you take a smaller salary or you go without being paid in order to meet other commitments. It is not always an easy road, but as long as it is really what you want to do, you will succeed. There is no pattern. You have to figure it out on your own. You learn as you go along. Everyone's experience is different. Occasionally you might be tempted to stop, but that's alright. We all get that feeling, yet we still continue. Once you love what you are doing, you will persevere.

Money matters keep you on your toes. Your expenditure is generally rent, electricity, telephone, gas, water, insurance, advertising, wages, packaging, tax, loan repayment, office and miscellaneous expenses, purchasing stock, general maintenance. Maintenance of the building is necessary. Have a good plumber, carpenter, mason, painter, tiler that you can call on any time.

The average business person can identify with most of these things. But paying rent, wages, insurance, tax, and utilities bills are major priorities. There is also that start-up cost. Whatever you make goes back into the business. In the beginning, I could barely pay myself a salary. The loan repayment was first and foremost for me, hence paying the loan back was a great accomplishment.

Operating on a tight budget, you should establish your primary objectives. You can get carried away and want to do many things all at once. If only you had the right amount of funds you would do this and that. My advice is to start with what you have. Limited funds stimulate creative thinking. There is that joyfulness deep inside when you make use of what is available. Pay attention to your overhead costs. Focus on cash flow. I kept detailed records, so I knew where money was coming from and where it was going.

Over the years I have learnt to stay out of debt. It allows me to be financially self-sufficient. How is that possible? I purchase the things I can afford. There is nothing like direct experience. I have been there before, and I know how I want to spend my life with money. Accumulating debt may cause you emotional or mental strain. It is better to deal with each money problem as it occurs and solve it. Make early payments. It leaves you with an inner peace and a calm feeling.

A reduced income should incite decreased spending. In other words, how much you spend is relative to your income. Keep your finances and spending balanced. It is better to adjust your lifestyle to suit your income. How does acquiring things beyond your reach enhance your life? You do not have to impress anyone. Is keeping up with the Joneses part of the budget?

You alone know how to tighten the shoes on your feet and can slacken them to make the adjustment for ease. Keep all your cost variables down at the level you can handle them. Money management is about regulating your funds for maximum benefit. It is relevant in both business and your personal life. How to budget, how to arrange your affairs and how to conduct your business are generally prime concerns. It often requires you to work with what you have. This practice is extremely useful. It helps you to avoid the financial pressures.

Be cost-conscious and compare prices when shopping. I shop around to be more cost effective. I can quote the different prices on the identical product at various stores, hence my children would often refer to me as the 'price guru'.

We often hear that we should pay ourselves first, but that is not always possible. Some months I didn't pay myself. Those times I told myself I was working for charity.

More lessons in business

Are you ready to take the rough with the smooth? Sometimes there is a shift in the foundation that shakes the earth from underneath you. Nevertheless, a business owner still has to control the day-to-day activities. Your reaction is fundamental to what is happening around you. There is a song by Peter Tosh which says 'I pick myself up, dust myself off and start all over again'. I listened to that song repeatedly until it sunk into my subconscious mind. I started afresh. I took matters into my own hands to uplift and sort out the business. I found that key and unlocked my door. Then I did everything I could think of to fill the void. Dedication would not let me give it up for anything on earth. Commitment eventually pays off.

What are you going to do about a situation that presents itself? Are you going to start over? Don't be afraid to start over. Most things in life move in cycles. Do not accept defeat. Keep going in spite of circumstances. Step forward and lift yourself up. A crisis has its own solution and you can find it. Meditate on the solution and turn your crisis into a resounding victory. You look for the positive in each day to celebrate. You have to trust you can win. Value yourself more. Know your value to the organization. When you put your heart and soul into the work, it is a glorious experience.

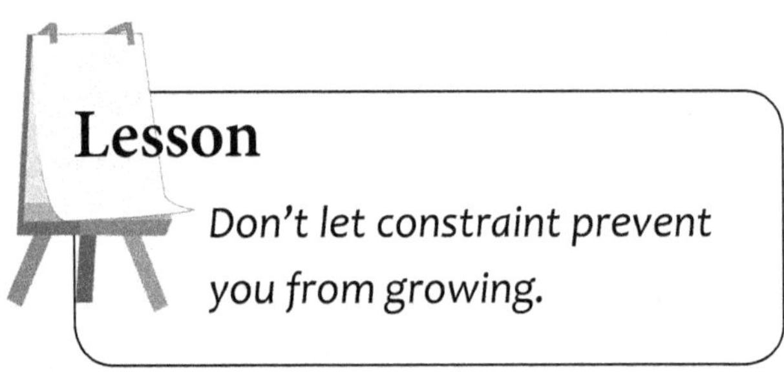

Lesson

Don't let constraint prevent you from growing.

A business owner should not be a myopic thinker. Be shrewd and vigilant in your business affairs. All your senses should be on alert. Exercise caution. I got played a couple of times. All the little signs were there, but I ignored what I was seeing. Be wary of ulterior motives and hidden agendas.

Make sound judgement of a situation and what is happening around you. However, in case you make a poor judgement, don't be hard on yourself. Get some benefit from it. Own your mistake. Every mistake helps you to grow.

Having your own business is indeed an experience with so many lessons. You have to know how to bridge those gaps and to fill those cracks that creep up slowly on you. It involves being realistic. There is no time to be pretentious. Have a clear understanding of what is really important.

As the owner you normally have to fill in for any temporary inconvenience. In an emergency, do not panic. Demonstrate that you know the work. Then there is that unforeseen circumstance at the time you felt everything was running smoothly. Do not be perturbed. Have the courage to face the unforeseen. We get by in spite of what happens. Somehow we find ways to remain well-grounded in the midst of turbulence, to remain focused regardless of the distractions, and remain strong no matter the responsibilities.

Don't settle for less. Picture your good. Look at the best way you can contribute and upscale the business. Create your own destiny and do it lovingly. Make it your own.

Words of wisdom

Don't concern yourself with what everybody is doing. What might work for them may not work for you. It varies from person to person. There is no overall pattern, only the specific pattern that fits what you want to accomplish. It is your vision. Be loyal to your vision. Own your uniqueness. You have to create your own style. You have to create your own brand.

Don't compare yourself to others. What is enough for you might not be enough for another person. What is acceptable to one person might be unacceptable to another. Be yourself. Self-awareness is vital.

Be conscious of the fact that we are in the same storm, but we are not in the same boat. Some have yachts while others have rowing boats. Nobody can fully understand another person's challenge. We may nod our heads in recognition or agreement, but who feels it knows it.

We may take a different approach in handling a particular concern. Different styles are appropriate for different situations. Each situation calls for a different response. Once you are satisfied and get the results you seek, then congratulations are in order.

We are all creative. There is nothing wrong with not following the crowd. Most of the great inventors did not adhere to what was thought to be normal. They experimented and did it their own way.

You have to know what works for you. Each of us brings our uniqueness to life. Adhering to your style is oftentimes more sensible. You alone know what you want to accomplish. You alone know how you want to invest your time, energy, talents and skills. You know what is best for you. 'Paddle your own canoe'

It is worthy to mention here that nobody can steal what is planted in your heart. I usually say, "I have no competition". The universe has enough for everyone. We do not have to compete. There is no need for the rival mentality. What we could do is to connect and encourage each other. We are all part of the web of life. We are all working to be successful. We all have that desire for prosperity.

Avoid conflicts and confrontations. You may have to resort to silence. Silence speaks. Silence gives you the time needed to iron out the discord by looking at it thoroughly.

Focus on what you did right. Compliment yourself.

Have one thing that brings some spark of delight within your being, even for just that moment to be merry.

Accept the things you cannot change. Have the courage to change the things you can and the wisdom to know the difference.

Do not repeat the same mistake over and over again. Liberate yourself by learning from it. Do not lower yourself to mediocre work. Aim high and do extraordinary things.

Avoid bluffing your way out when responding to a question during any conversation. You never know who you are speaking with. That individual might be quite proficient on the subject. Saying you do not know gives you the opportunity to learn something new. Every person you meet is a teacher in some form.

There are some folks who seem to have all the answers about everything. Do not be quick or hasty to judge unless you have walked in another person's shoes. Have a listening ear. Listen without judgment. Be more understanding and accepting to others.

Letter to the Aspiring Entrepreneur

Self-employment is totally different to working for somebody. You go beyond the call of duty. You still turn up even if you are feeling under the weather. Actually, if you don't show up there is no money coming in. If you send no ship out, no ship will come in.

Many mornings I ask myself: "Why am I doing this again?" But at the end of the day I give thanks for holding on and keeping the business alive, and give gratitude for customers' support. As I keep going my strength grows. Every day is a second chance. Every day has possibilities. Be open to those possibilities. Every step gets you there. Although things may seem hard, still keep your vision. Every new day brings opportunity. Always give appreciation for all that you have accomplished along the way.

Honour your word, be reliable and be punctual. These are good traits to possess. Furthermore, build your business on a foundation of honesty and trust.

Be self-reliant. Explore deeper. Relearning and reinventing can advance your personal growth. Only you know what is best for yourself. Only you know what you want. Only you know what is exciting to you. Keep your goal clear, embrace it, and live it.

Running a business requires effective cost control. Once you have enough space at home, I suggest you start there first. Only you can decide what suits you best, but the high cost of operating from a commercial building was certainly enough reason for me to become home-based. It resolves the headaches of having all those monthly expenses. If there is less income you don't have the huge overheads to worry about.

Your light may dim occasionally, but let that not inhibit you. In other words, when the going gets tough, see it through and stand firm. It shows you who you are. Continue until things fall into place. Who knows what is out there waiting for you to show up?

You have goals and therefore assessment of the business is necessary. It shows you what is working and what is not. It helps you to see what progress has been made and if you have reached your specific objectives. They can be affected by a number of external and internal factors. The business may not always be doing as you would like. Set targets you can achieve in the day-to-day action. This helps eliminate frustration.

Should you go to plan B when plan A is not producing as you had projected? Only you can decide, but whatever the decision, put your plan into action and give it your all. Focus on making things better. In the meanwhile, feel great about any accomplishment until things come together.

Sometimes you do not get the break you would have preferred, but it is what you do with what you have that gives you that push. Utilize what is on hand. Work with what you have available at that specific moment. Fuel up with more energy so that you can accomplish your dreams. Keep walking even if you have to travel the path alone. It is your own growth. Stay with what is right.

Sincerely, Augustina.

Happy Memories: The Middle Years

Vegan Conscious books on display at the National Independence Festival of Creative Arts night event.

Lise from Denmark, and Shelley Carrington who has been patronizing the business for several years.

Lise and Bo with friends Beverly and Paul Hadchity and Karen from US.

Marjorie Riley celebrating with her family at her 86th birthday celebration.

Vegan Cottage. A healthier way of life.

The exterior of Vegan Cottage. Eating here is an experience to remember. It is family-friendly where all are welcome, and offer something for everyone. Whether you are dining in or taking out we provide tempting, tasty nutritious meals.

The interior of Vegan Cottage. It is a comfortable environment in which you can eat, drink and relax with multiple settings. Either as a group or just to sit down and dine with people you don't know yet. It is also ideal for special functions and business lunches. It has a peaceful atmosphere for unwinding.

Makila and her family from Trinidad are among those who have dined with us.

Lise and Bo from Denmark have been coming to Barbados for over 23 years. They are repeat visitors to Vegan Cottage. "A Home away from Home."

A night at Vegan Cottage with the international students from the Bellairs Research Institute of McGill University. Located at Folkestone, St. James, Barbados.

International students from Bellairs at Vegan Cottage.

International students from Bellairs at Vegan Cottage.

Semyon (in the light blue shirt), the group coordinator with fellow students from Bellairs.

International students from Bellairs at Vegan Cottage.

International students from Bellairs at Vegan Cottage.

The parents of some international students relaxing after dinner.

Me and International students from the University of the West Indies Cave Hill.

My son Shomari and I with Daniele Debbi.

An unforgettable evening at this teachers' celebration.

Heather Ward (fourth from left) with other teachers as they make a toast to each other.

Jessica Spingola from Montreal.

Hearty lunchtime get together for these workmates at Vegan Cottage.

Tatjana Trebic from Canada.

Zdravka, who is
Tatjana's mum.

You and the Product

You have the product, what next?

Let us look at some fundamental questions. Who are you targeting? Is the business catering for everybody? How do you choose the right target audience? Do you have a high quality product? Are you looking at volume?

Is the price affordable? Can it be adjusted to oblige that individual who is low on funds? Sticking out for a price can at times be pointless. A business owner has to know when to adopt a more pliant attitude and listen to the customer's request.

Location is important. Do you have an ideal location? Is it easily accessible to human traffic? Take into account the availability of public transport or a taxi service. Is there adequate parking for the customer? Is the location in close proximity to other commercial activities? Furthermore, is it in close proximity to where you can purchase raw materials and other necessities? My location is central. I am about a few kilometres from the city, which is convenient, as I have access to numerous things. In addition I am situated near to the farmer's market, grocery and wholesale stores.

Is your product needed for the specific time you are in? Do a trial run to see the response you get. The marketing strategy should be designed to encourage the use of the product and should highlight its benefits. What are your marketing strategies?

The name you give to the business is paramount. It should indicate what you are doing. Have a name that describes the product. There should be no guessing about what you are offering.

Take pride in your working environment. People like to be in an establishment which is clean, tidy and has attractive décor.

Marketing your product

You have a product. How are you going to market it?

You should know everything possible about your product. If not you, then who? Once you are knowledgeable about the product you are able to provide useful information. You can educate people on its benefits and advantages. Potential buyers look out for their best interests and tend to listen to that person who is eloquent and knows their stuff.

Everyone who comes your way is a potential customer. Take advantage of that opportune moment to market your product. You may be operating from a table on the street, a van, under a tent, or a store. No matter where, you are your business. First impressions count and are long lasting. A person always remembers your warm greeting, pleasant manners and professional service.

Engage with that customer. Let them know what you do and the service you are offering. I call it connecting with the buyer. Be enthusiastic about the item you are selling. Speak with gusto in your voice. Your love for the product shows and helps sell it. Resort to the topic that you know well. It allows you to speak with confidence.

Take advantage of every occasion to market your product. Be polite and courteous to everyone, whether in person or on the phone. Good manners can help sell your product. The common decency within you says much about your character.

How is your product presented? Presentation of the product is crucial for winning over the buyer. Let your set-up be impressive in order to get someone's attention. Are you looking for new customers? Then have a captivating display. We buy with our eyes.

I find that personal selling is more feasible for promoting products. To reach a wider market I attended galas and festival events where thousands of people were gathered. I was able to see directly how the market responded to my product.

I also did sampling promotions at supermarkets, which was good exposure. In addition, there were seminars that were health-oriented. At these functions my audience was mostly health conscious individuals who were looking for alternatives to improve their eating habits. The environment was perfect to test out the product. At company exhibitions and fairs I took that advantage to display my product. I participated in trade shows where agents were advertising new lines of healthy items.

How to be on top of the game

Be knowledgeable in the field of work you have chosen. Educate yourself; do research. Be more than good at your craft—master it. Practice makes the expert. Acquire new skills. Never stop improving and building your personal assets. Be up-to-date with the latest trends. Don't be caught napping. Although you may have a premium product, do not become complacent. Keep learning and finding ways to expand your knowledge.

I constantly obtain trending material to read. Reading helps you to accumulate information. Subscribe to magazines and newsletters. They usually have interesting articles. Have all types of books on various topics, especially those pertaining to your area of work.

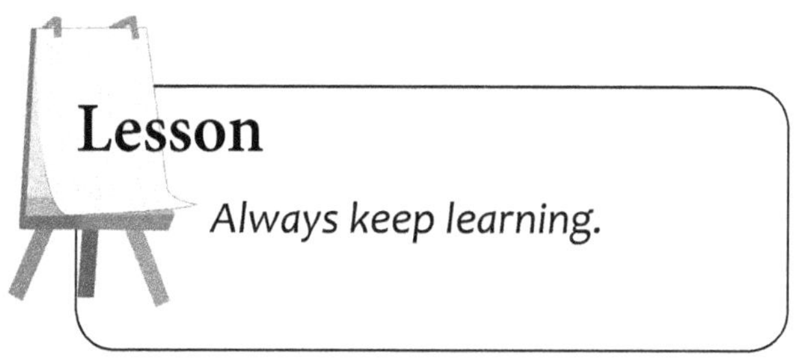

We are all creators in our own right. We can tap into our unlimited supplies. Discover your potential, for you have so much to offer. Produce to make this world a better place. We are our prime resource. We have the potential to invent superior things and as I write, new ones are being discovered. These discoveries have created an excitement for incorporating them into our daily lifestyle.

The speed at which information is shared has increased in recent years. Getting things done is faster. This is a new era and things are constantly changing. We have to keep up. Internet technology has impacted on the way we now do things compared to how we did them years ago. For example, there is digital marketing, online advertising, online buying and online banking.

Information is more readily accessible, thus allowing business personnel to have instant news. We are blessed to be alive in this internet age.

In today's sophisticated technological times, many things are occurring rapidly. Stay in touch with the changes and you will be on top of the game. Be prepared to adapt to changes in the environment. Watch the trends and strategize. Keep your ears to the ground. Listen to conversations to get a sense of what's happening out there in the business world. It is up to you to hear and to respond to what's going on around you.

Simply market to your existing customers

It is upmost to maintain excellent customer service. Be consistent with what you are producing. Quality speaks for itself and brings the repeat customer. Give a service that would leave people with a sense of satisfaction. Satisfied customers bring their friends and family.

The service you are providing within the market should be top-notch. Your service helps sell your product. Use customer feedback to assist you in gauging how you are performing. Feedback informs you about your performance level. Implement new methods if necessary to make the product better and better. Go beyond your normal. Have an improved look; fancier packaging could very well be the catch.

I find that word-of-mouth is the unrivaled advertising tool. Let me repeat: word-of-mouth is the best means of advertising. It works! When a new face shows up I always ask: "Who told you about us?" The referral is usually from an existing customer or another business. Glowing reviews online also sold the experience of eating at the restaurant and helped bring more customers. Great marketing attracts people. If your product serves people well they will come back to your establishment.

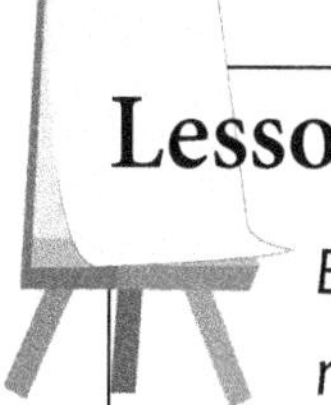

Lesson

Excellent service builds your reputation.

Building strong
client relationships

The value of the client to your business is important. I am happy when my clients are happy. Happiness is connected to satisfaction.

Make people feel important and loved. Long term relationships are inevitable when you make them feel valued and appreciated. It is worthy to mention here that personalized service is unforgettable. For instance, simply remembering that person's name and their preferences makes a huge difference. Go the extra mile to be thoughtful and attentive while you are providing a service. The reaction to gentleness is favourable.

Give superior customer service and the result is a loyal customer. Keeping in touch is another way of providing exceptional service. A telephone call is received with much glee. Stay connected with your clients. Have a close rapport. Check up on your clients once they are ill. A visit is nice. It deepens client relationships. Taking good care of your client reaps great benefits.

Treat people with respect. Be kind and loving in your approach. It brings goodwill to the business. A good relationship with the client is essential. Have a pleasant demeanour so that the client feels welcome in your presence. Greet everyone who you come into contact with each day at the workplace with love. Have a reassuring smile on your face. Create a climate for friendliness and the behaviour of people is admirable.

Create an atmosphere where people who enter feel peaceful, joyful, and loving energy. It comes with the whole package. Be genuine, honest and sincere.

People are drawn to others who make them feel better about themselves. A kind remark gives pleasure. Brighten someone's day by saying encouraging and complimenting words. Have a great day! You look fabulous! You never know what is happening in their lives and those words can very well be the antidote. Tell your clients how much you appreciate their patronage. That kind of gesture radiates pure love. Your charisma or charm is an asset to the business.

Harness your customer's goodwill. Buy and use your customers' products and tell others about them. Patronize the services they offer.

Twists and turns

Some people say the 'best is yet to come', but I say live your best every day. We make all types of plans and then there are twists and turns. How did I handle the twists and turns? I looked around and realized that I still have so much to give thanks for. I took my own advice and I stayed open to the change. I followed my heart and traveled into the unknown and discovered so many things about operating a business and about myself. I opened every door. I continue to learn and grow.

The goal is to continue, moving from one level to another, going higher and higher. Let us be inspired and enlightened during our journey—a journey rich and full of goodness of things we could imagine. Let us in our search embrace the ultimate. Let us analyze each of the turns. Today I give thanks for all those turns which have moved me from strength to strength. Your will power and your courage become unceasing.

I must emphasize that in peace and silence we find answers. There is always an answer.

It is how we face the twists and turns in our lives that determines our outlook on life. Set up your system and make things work. The twists and turns bring a wealth of understanding about life. They brought me to writing my thoughts. Writing is a form of meditation for me. I am in love with writing. I am at my happiest when I am writing.

It gives me joy. What gives you the greatest joy? Unearth the thing that brings you gladness.

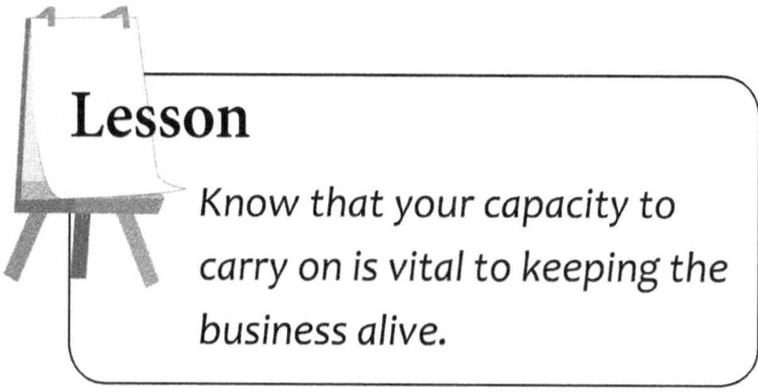

Lesson

Know that your capacity to carry on is vital to keeping the business alive.

Courage is currency

The daily operation of a business takes diligence in order to accomplish whatever you need it to be. Astuteness is necessary, for it has to be profitable. Owning a business, you have to take care of numerous things. Business life can be hectic and still be enjoyable.

To say I did not feel disappointed once in a while would be an untruth. But the vision kept me going. The call was that deep and I liked what I was doing. I am satisfied with the things I have done with my talent, skills and knowledge. The journey was long, tiring at times, but I also had fun. At some stages there was playfulness and I am amused at how it has evolved. Now I have a story I can share.

In the beginning you are a little apprehensive and

you have a fluttering sensation in your stomach. You are venturing into the unknown, but after you get started that feeling disappears. When you first start out your business, it is like a baby needing special attention and watchfulness. Be mentally prepared for early mornings and late nights. To get things done you might have less sleep. In the initial stage it has to be constantly nourished, but eventually it gets to the weaning stage. A business thrives with love and care. Make it all worth living the dream.

The difficulties help us to know our capabilities

From time to time tiredness would creep in, but when I told myself I was not tired, a burst of energy usually came. Then I got to work out that not dwelling on what I was feeling but focusing on what I wanted to achieve shut down the fatigue. I could not stop until I was finished and somehow I got enough energy to complete. We know our strengths and the length we can go. Little by little we can make it work.

I kept on at all costs despite the long hours and continuous work. Yes, there were sleepless nights too, but I got through them. I am glad I kept at it. When I completed a task there was that awesome feeling, like a burst of jubilation. There have been times when I literally uttered a cry of joy.

Most times when I felt tired I found the mental power to carry the load. It was implanted deep within my heart. Let persistence and determination get you through to accomplish your purpose. I can see how they relate to reaching every milestone in my business.

I continued to work tirelessly. It was my Spirit that enabled me to be triumphant. Through self-examination I was able to ask the question: "What purpose am I truly here for?" I listened to my innermost being which revealed my soul's chosen path. It is my calling and I answer the call in any way possible. Every day is different. You have to find that meaning in the day and see what it is telling you. Do not disregard the meaning.

I stop and give thanks for life; for being able to advance. I give thanks for finding ways to succeed and persistence to continue even when I do not know the outcome. Be unattached to the outcome and feed your dream to help it grow. A farmer takes care of the crops, likewise a proprietor takes care of the business. Both are trusting that all their efforts will be worthwhile. It teaches us about ourselves without attachment to the outcome.

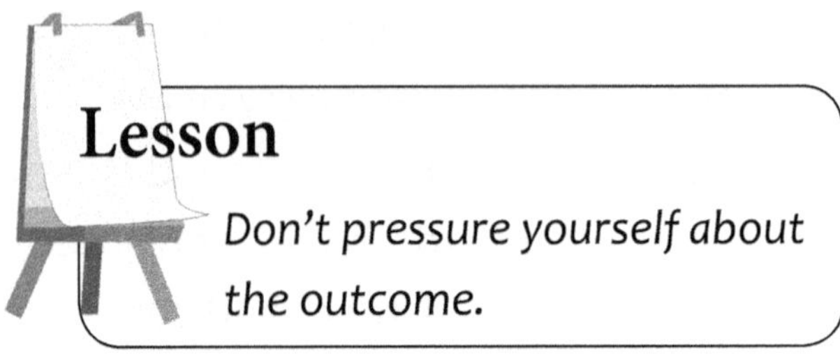

Are you going to press ahead? Risk losing to have more freedom? Reduce the amount of work load? The decision is strictly yours. In a nutshell, business is about making decisions. Be accountable for your actions. Take the initiative and serve the moment. Reorganize yourself. There is a reason for most things.

Life is full of mysteries

We are all searching for some meaning, but life is full of mysteries. I am of the opinion that we are guided by our own situations. As the mysteries unfold we get a clearer understanding of what is going on and what life is telling us.

I remembered when I was in primary school the teacher wrote on the board "Cleanliness is next to Godliness". Something about the statement caught my attention at that young age. I wanted to understand what Godliness was all about. The longing to know grew as I got older. Finally, I came to the realization that Godliness is everywhere. I saw it in nature. I detected it in people. I felt it in songs. I noticed it in poetry. I observed it in dance. I felt it in the silence. Godliness is in your own being. It is not separate. Godliness is an awareness. It is an experience.

Joy is in Godliness

Peace is in Godliness

Love is in Godliness

We seek, but whatever we want is already there. Stop seeking too much. Greatness resides within you. Go within and discover your greatness. You are already enough. Accept where you are in life and make the most of every day. Every day brings distinct messages. Simply listen. Adhere to silence and listen to the small voice. In quietness the answer comes.

Embrace the positive

On and off, we spend our time worrying about the small stuff and the bigger picture is there in full view. There is no point in worrying daily; it is not good for mental health. It is up to us to renounce the worries. Focus on what actually works. It is also not necessary to struggle. Stop struggling and experience serenity. Dwell on the good happening around you. The seed is planted in the right soil. Let it grow.

One day I decided to stop worrying. The worry became joy. One day I decided to stop struggling. The struggle became peace.

How to approach obstacles and problems

Trust in yourself to solve the problem. Trust removes hesitancy. Be your best where you are. Feel good about yourself. Do the best you can and adjust yourself in the situation. It is up to you to make whatever you want out of life. Do your work with much love. When you do your work with much zest despite the obstacles, you can see them through. Have might to tackle whatever obstacle comes your way. Obstacles pull everything out of us. Then we know who we truly are.

The key is to picture your success. Life is about being creative. Therefore, look for creative solutions to your problem. Let problems become motivation for creations. Further, confront your problems and learn to solve them. We must solve our own problems. The solutions are in the problems.

The wisest course of action is to face the problem directly. Don't run away from it. The testing of your problems produces self-mastery.

Detachment

It is wise to relinquish all worn out things and unpleasantness in the establishment. Clear away the negativity. It transforms your life and you are happier and peaceful on the inside. Become cognizant of what matters and what works. Let go of what no longer works. Release things you no longer need. Let go of what no longer serves you.

Whatever has happened, has happened. Don't put pressure on yourself. The door that remains shut is usually for some reason. What I am explaining here is that another door opens eventually. The universe is full of life. Every day there is something to look forward to. When I arrive home each day after work I realize how much I have to give thanks for.

Family life with business

I am a restaurateur managing the business and taking care of my family. Juggling between the two is taxing at times, for both need my full attention. You must be careful in order not to affect your loved ones at home. You also must be careful lest you burn the candle at both ends and burn yourself out. You have to be nurturing and understanding. You have to provide emotional and physical care. You have to be thorough. But you still have to be independent and responsible for your wellbeing. All of these certainly call for ingenuity and flexibility.

When building up the business, long hours are often required. Early mornings and late nights are involved. You might have to schedule specific times that do not overlap with your family affairs. There are continuous demands and you must have the tenacity to direct your way through them. In addition, it usually calls for making numerous decisions. You are responsible for your own decisions.

More than once I was tempted to quit, but I resisted the temptation. I told myself I will not give up. Giving up was not an option. I placed my hand on my chest and I felt the rhythm of my heartbeat.

As I listened I was conscious that I was alive. In that moment I was reminded that everything was alright.

As a business owner, to be able to juggle between work and my personal life I had to learn how to say 'no'. Establish what is truly important to you and disregard irrelevant distractions. Note that proper management of your time is essential.

I organized and prioritized my day to maintain productivity at the restaurant and the general responsibilities that came with family life. It usually calls for multi-tasking. There is something about multi-tasking that makes me feel good about myself. You take on the characteristics of being assertive, creative, and less dependent, and you tend to be more confident.

Is it possible to both take care of a business and family and still create the life you want? Yes. The key is finding a balance for personal fulfillment and being content with your life. Your balance brings light and joy. Taking care of yourself and family are closely intertwined. We are all connected; none exists without the other. On the other hand, your work and personal life may clash occasionally. To find balance you might have to transform your mind-set. Your strength depends on it. It can be complicated at times, but eventually you figure out how to put the pieces together.

Work needs to be in balance with your personal life. I just had to find balance, for there was no manual or handbook I could pick up that would give me an immediate answer. Most of the time I trusted my Intuition. Balance involves being mentally, emotionally, spiritually and physically stable. How do you know when there is balance? Balance brings instant peace.

I maintain balance by going into relaxation mode. It eases tension in my body. This practice releases what I am experiencing externally. At that moment I feel an inner peace—there is a rich peace inside, no matter what is happening around you.

Coping mechanisms

On occasion I would take a pause when work got too demanding and read a few uplifting quotes. Humming or singing kept me placid as I worked. I also listened to mellow music. The music in my soul soothed me. The music in my Spirit helped me to continue. The music in my heart cheered me on. The music in my mind let me knew it was going to be fine, that I was able and I would make it. The music was therapeutic. It brought calmness. It kept me composed and unruffled. I curled up with a book or watched a movie. I became engrossed in my preferred hobby—crossword puzzles—which helped to declutter my mind.

I also read something inspiring just before going to sleep, and when I woke up. I retreated to a secluded area, giving thanks for what I have received. My coping mechanism set in and there was relief.

When you need a break, just take it. We all need a break to unwind and to rest; to get away from the daily routine—a time to be quiet, to make space for you, to enjoy your own company.

There is always something to rescue the day, to lift you up when you can't hold on any longer. It could be delightful memories. Find solace in whatever gives you comfort and ease. Stop and relax. In stillness the body is recharged, the energy flows, ideas come and creativity rises.

Do what's in your heart. Do what you do with excellence and feel great about your acts. Business helps you to support your lifestyle and to grow as a person.

We are all managing even if it is in different ways. You know what makes you tick. You have to do what is necessary to succeed. Create your own formula and take charge. Know that you are born to win.

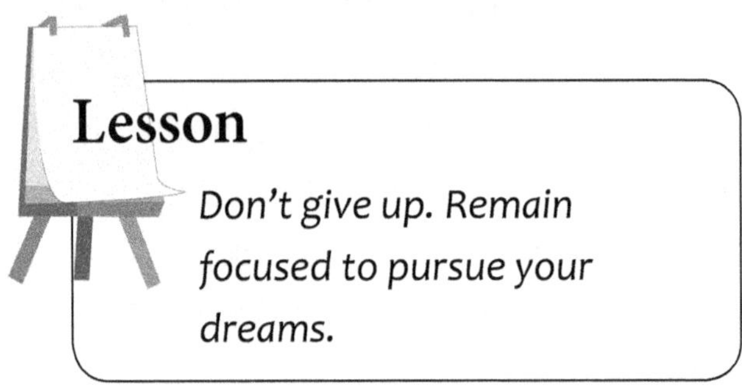

Time management and motion

Motion study was an elective at college, and I found that knowledge to be useful in the business. It is about the best methods of doing work to minimize the amount of movement. It helps preserve energy and decreases unnecessary motion. Note that in restaurant service you are always back and forth with customers. Have a layout at the workplace that would help to eliminate wasteful movement, save time, and still foster productivity.

I set up my workstation to avoid unnecessary movement. It is about how I pace myself. Things are strategically placed to lessen fatigue and to give ease to make the work load lighter. What I use frequently is close to hand. It prevents me from scurrying around. The objective is to reduce movement, thus preserve energy and hinder exhaustion.

Why is time management necessary? It simply saves time. It allows you to accomplish more daily in order to get you through every day and carry the business to the next level. You must be well organized. Structure your work hours, set priorities and use your time wisely. Advanced preparation is helpful. It stops you from being too rushed.

Managing your time properly might call for arranging your duties accordingly. You can have productive time and quiet time. Manage your time and take breaks during work to let the body regenerate.

I keep my clock at least ten minutes fast. It allows me to get a head start. When you are pressed for time it is wiser to put your energy into the most important thing. Know what your time is worth.

Success

How do you view success? Is it having your own business? Is it about accomplishing what you set out to do? How do you measure success? Is it about the money? Are you swayed by profit? Is it about amassing wealth? Are you enjoying peace, health and love? Are you contented? What does success mean to you?

When you have done your best you are successful. Be pleased with your achievements in business or in life. Enjoy your success and continual progress. Success is also about joy and happiness in totality; a revelation of wholeness in mind, body, soul and Spirit.

Growth happens when you are prepared to do the work. It may cause you to work longer hours. Growth happens when you continue despite all that is happening around you. You have that choice to make it work by doing it your own way.

There is a deep desire to perform my best at whatever I do. This fire arouses my soul. I knew what I wanted to project so I put in the extra effort daily. Being committed to the cause was important to me. It kept me centred. Enthusiasm kept me going and helped me to accomplish what I was going after.

Find a niche in your field and offer excellent service. Invent your own business and work in the area you most enjoy. Choose to do something you love. Become an expert by focusing on what you do better to come up with favourable results. Life takes us through several paths. Be aware of what is possible and travel the path you have chosen.

The unexplainable

When I reflect on my life I realize there were moments when whatever I needed at that particular time was given to me. It could be moral support, financial support or physical support—assistance comes when we need it.

I remember the time my co-worker was on a week's sick leave. What was I going to do? As I was pondering my next move, someone came through the restaurant door, saw me working by myself and asked if I needed help. He was a restaurant manager. I was in awe. We worked beautifully together for three days. The precise help always turns up when you need it. It is as if the universe saw your sticky situation and responded. I leave it to the reader to decide if this was a blessing, a meaningful coincidence, or both.

Oftentimes we are guided to what we need intuitively. It was the fifth anniversary of the restaurant and I was looking for dinner plates. I had a specific type in mind. I went to quite a few stores, but didn't see anything I liked. As I was about to go home the car broke down outside a hardware store. It was an inconvenience, but it worked out perfectly. I walked into that store and there were the plates I wanted.

It was a Sunday evening and I went to a lecture. The address was being given by a prominent motivational speaker. He spoke about empowerment and enfranchisement, which were pertinent to entrepreneurs. His delivery was powerful and convincing. Somehow I knew that after that speech I would get the financial assistance I sought. The person in charge of making that happen came up the stairs and sat next to me during part of the presentation. Just walk your path no matter what happens. Life usually works out.

Your guides will appear to assist you throughout the journey. During my teaching career, a tutor from the Hospitality Institute gave an educational talk to the students about the courses offered there. As I listened to her, the area of food service attracted me. I felt a strong urge to pursue this line of study, and I applied. However, at the interview one of the interviewers suggested I should study Hotel Management and Institutional Catering instead. I took his advice. The course was well-rounded and covered a wide range of subjects. Little did I know that it was preparing me for where I am now.

Life has a way of bringing us to the right place. The building I rented had the exact design I wanted for the restaurant. A bank had been in that location before and everything was correctly in position. Hence the previous manager's office became a cozy dining area; the workers' lunch room was transformed into the kitchen; the vault was used as the storeroom. In addition, there were plenty of cupboards under the counter top. Electrical sockets were installed everywhere possible. There was adequate floor-space to accommodate the furniture and equipment.

A pattern of synchronicity was in the unexplainable events that occurred in my life. Divine guidance is available to us, and reassures us that we are on the right path. I am aware that it has assisted in my development.

Feel great knowing that life is full of blessings and favours. Life can take us to the imaginable. Life is just for living. Love yourself and experience life as it unfurls its mysteries and wonders. Appreciate the offerings and embrace the joys. For who knows, the unexpected turns up and our wants are provided each day without effort. Remember, you were helped in some way.

Tested

Tests are not about the absence of difficulties, but the ability to rise above them. We all have been tested at some point in our lives, hence we know what to do and how to do it. Don't let the testing dictate your advancement. Stand the test of time. Have self-confidence. Things generally work out.

I was tested, but the stronger part of me took over. I came closer to light, and I got a glimpse of why I was born. I asked myself many questions as I was being tested. Some I could answer, others I left alone.

How did I keep the door open all these years? I had the growth mindset that I am my business and my business is me. The product is part of me. We are a package. Nothing can come between us. Nothing can break us. Furthermore, I have a mission. It is not easy to shake it off. The feeling is too strong. It would not let me leave. It's in my heart, my soul; it doesn't go anywhere. It is in my DNA.

In the beginning I wrote a mission statement for my business. It is my guide. Why do I go on and on? I have too many years invested in the dream. I have come too far to walk away. I continue to bring about these things planted into my soul, my being. I have work to do and I can fulfill it. I am depending on me to preserve myself and in the process live to see the outcome. The anchor which has sustained me and kept me going is still working—the power to be; the power to do; the power to reach the full essence of life; to inspire myself; to overcome and know it after performing so many things. By persevering you inspire others.

How do we live in these uncertain times? We must do whatever we are called to do with commitment and leave a trail of goodness. We must function on a higher plane. We must give gratitude for all we have achieved in spite of what is happening. We must give thanks for all those individuals who help in whatever way to keep our businesses open. Reflect on your blessings.

Focus on the good things. Be happy with the good you did throughout the day. Rendering a service brings cheerfulness. The passion that lies deep within gets you through. The wisdom accumulated from previous events gives the ability to strive for success. Remember that you were in similar situations and you still made it. Patience works it out. The sun disappears beneath the clouds for a little while, but know that the sun eventually shows.

Every day is a fresh beginning. Give thanks for the sales you receive. Bless them. Give thanks for your customers. Bless them. Bless your works continually. What you bless you multiply.

In times of uncertainty, don't be swayed from your vision. Know that life is full of endless opportunities. We are all facing something in life. You are not alone. A door closes and you have to open another. Find your superpower. Dare to undertake something new to see how it works.

Sit quietly and listen attentively. The peace in listening gives you the extra drive.

The wisdom gained from over 25 years of my life in the restaurant business is awe-inspiring. I am thankful for reaching every milestone. It was tiring at times, but I had the endurance to handle what confronted me. The wide knowledge outweighs all those tiresome days.

Thanks to the most powerful Supreme who has kept me through it all. Thanks for preserving me during those years. You have helped me maintain my sanity and I did not break/falter from the pressure. I recall swamp days, but I felt God's presence urging me on until it became alright.

I know what I have withstood. These days I just live, thanking the Creator for the breath of life. When the day is finished I give thanks for life. I give thanks for the sales. I give thanks for my supportive clients. I must emphasize here that the key is giving thanks. To tell the truth, it is what has kept me all these years. The fact that I passed the trials and have gathered more strength and wisdom to keep the business going, that's why I give the most thanks.

I got tired from time to time, but not frustrated, as my soul's core knew my mission and kept pulling me. I found my purpose and life had a true meaning.

I wonder

Sometimes I wonder about the time. I feel that time may be passing. But then I realize that time is not my controller. I am the driving force and I can make it happen. Do not create anxiety for yourself. Why bother yourself about time? There is always enough time. There is no limit to time.

Sometimes I wonder if it is all worth it. To quell this feeling I would give thanks for the marvellous things in my life, then I feel great and know for sure it is worth it. Was it worth it? Yes it was, just to be able to write a book like this.

Sometimes I wonder about the ending because doubt likes to creep in once in a while. I tell myself I am fully equipped to handle and I can manage. The doubt disappears. You have to be able to disregard any doubts and go forward. Yes I had doubts, but I remained true to the cause.

Sometimes I wonder if I would take this path again. There were some drawbacks, but nothing can replace the wisdom I acquired and the beautiful people I met. Experiences and memories live on. I found my own path and followed it. You learn something every day. You go on discovering. There is so much to explore.

When nothing seems to be happening the way you envisioned it, at some point you have to ease off and be still. You cannot wave a wand and think everything that you do not like or approve of will magically disappear. Be still.

Peaks and valleys

There are peaks and valleys in the journey. The valleys taught me how I could do better. They helped me to acknowledge that I am the pilot of my own life. During the bumpiest path in the journey I saw the things that were necessary for my advancement. Sometimes valleys may be just what is needed to rejuvenate your life. As you progress, the 'aha moment' comes and you realized you were preparing yourself all along.

Life lessons are life blessings.

The peaks can be insightful. They showed me

that my labour was not in vain. The peaks are indications that there are more channels available for our prosperity.

We all learn from each other

We learn something from everyone who passes through our lives, however minor or major it may seem. At some point in our lives we are teachers and we are students. What I am referring to does not apply to being in the classroom. We all meet for some reason. We may not understand it at that particular time, but we all gain from each other.

I can remember going to a function where the owners were celebrating 25 years in business. I was impressed with the whole event, and decided I would reach that milestone too. I kept telling myself that I would go the distance. It's amazing how your life can be influenced by what you see or hear.

I can recall sayings which have impacted on my life. My recurring clients would say little things which were 'food for thought' and stayed with me. Junior's phrase was "to whom much is given, much is required". The meaning of his statement became clearer as I got on with life. Pat said to me "August, when one is sowing another is reaping".

I retained this in my mind and prepared myself for harvesting time. Stay put until the harvest starts to come in.

Jordan's saying was "more money cannot be going out than what is coming in". He was absolutely correct. Harold would ever so often remark "everything comes with a price" and as the years roll on I have come to understand what he meant. I certainly paid the price. What price are you willing to pay? It could be either financial, physical, mental, emotional, or all occurring at the same time.

Many of my clients are business owners, so I am privileged to have a forum to share experiences. I recognize that their stories are quite similar to my own. Our chief concern is generally keeping the business afloat during stormy waters. Knowing that the business is stable in spite of trials gives us a sort of security. Our tireless effort is testimony to our devotion.

We plant our seeds and wait for them to burst open. We watch them grow until they mature into something beautiful.

We tend to gravitate towards people who share our same interests. I am glad to have such people in my life. We have constructive conversations about what is happening in the food industry and business economy. We discuss what we are experiencing and exchange ideas. We encourage each other. We offer each other support.

Welcome love in whatever fashion it occurs. It is comforting to have that one person who offers fervent support—someone who listens and is willing to help you deal with issues.

Show clemency to your fellow human beings. Do not let the pressures of the business ever cause you to be unkind. Being kind-hearted gives a great feeling. Let things you do be for good; a goodness that comes from deep within. In life, as long as we remain compassionate and loving, we would have done well. Love, peace, joy and compassion bring sweetness to the soul.

How it all started

After I finished my studies in Hotel Management and Institutional Catering, it took me about 15 years before I opened the restaurant. I am convinced it had to do with timing. It was the perfect time. People were beginning to take a keen interest in their wellness. They were going to gyms and looking for other ways to improve their health.

I started catering first to the people in my neighbourhood, offering lunches on weekends and providing delivery services to other areas. I also had booths at various functions. The comments were encouraging, which helped give birth to the restaurant.

I was excited about the product—Vegan Cuisine—I was bringing to the market. Vegan was part of my lifestyle and what I was passionate about. I could help people by advocating a healthier way of life. There was a need for this type of restaurant. People were gravitating towards healthy living, and being conscious of how they ate. It created an excitement for incorporating more plant-based foods into their diets. This crave was on the rise and it gave me the opportunity to use my talents to the fullest.

Take advantage of an opportunity when it presents itself. I created my own work by utilizing my skill and knowledge. In fact, it is more than talent or skill. It is discernment. I consider it as my work and not a job. The work is a part of my spiritual quest. Our talent is a gift we can share with others.

I was catering to everyone, whether vegan or not. My emphasis was on top-notch presentation and superior quality; providing tasty, nutritious meals in a homely and friendly atmosphere. I wanted to dismiss the notion that consumption of these foods was boring and monotonous. The concept worked. The word of what I was doing spread and there was a surge of people wanting to try the menu. Although I was specializing in vegan cuisine, I was also focusing on total well-being and good health.

Take your vision and bring it to actual existence. You should take the opportunities that arise.

It was a giant step to venture into opening a restaurant. Whether it was celebrating the 5th, 10th, 15th, 20th, or 25th year, each milestone was significant to my personal development. However, the 25th anniversary was momentous, as it marked a specific point in my field of work, for I had traveled the distance.

Step by step, I made it because I got up every morning wanting to conquer all things. At every major step my strength and courage increased. Each milestone was a moment of thanksgiving to mark the advancement in my work

Some of my glorious years were having one-on-one interactions with my clients and discussing the connection with vegan and health. Another highlight was to teach vegan cuisine at workshops. I was in my element and I loved it. Knowing I am doing something worthwhile brings a feeling words cannot explain. Assisting others makes your day more meaningful. Give, and life gives you back.

Health and wellness

The amount of time you spend with the business to make everything right can affect your personal life. The day to day grind can be too much. You can become overworked. There were days when I was so stretched that I scarcely had spare time for myself. I knew that this was not a healthy practice, and I was going down the wrong road. I had to set aside some quality time for myself to replenish my Spirit. You don't have to be busy all the time. Know what deserves your time and energy, and what does not.

You have to be obedient to your health. Your health is important in every area of your life. There is no substitute for good health. Set boundaries that work for you. Make changes as you see fit. You have to know when it is enough. You can do something about it. Your health is what you envisage it to be. You can take your destiny in your hands.

Learn how to destress before the pressure builds up. Find time for yourself. Find time for mindfulness. Find time to rest and enjoy the beauty around you. Bring sunshine into your life.

Healthy thoughts and being conscious of that higher power within go hand in hand. Live every minute with love and gratitude. Live in the present and you are at peace.

Take care of your body. Maintain health by consuming more wholesome foods. Exercise. You have to know when it is time to slow down and set aside quiet moments for yourself. Put whatever is happening on hold. Invest in your wellness. Do something different. Add spice to your life. Take a vacation. Take time to enjoy what you worked steadily for. Go on that cruise you have been promising yourself.

Use upbeat affirmations daily. It registers in the subconscious. Have a healthy outlook on life, as emotions and thoughts can affect the immune system. How we react to our wellness is important. By your actions you see love; by your words you hear love; and by your touch you feel love. Let love bring a sweet aroma of joy, peace and happiness wherever you are. Let love penetrate your soul and your being. It is part of healthy living.

A life-changing experience

Every morning I wake up as early as 3 o'clock. It is peaceful. There are fewer distractions. It is more productive. I could walk to work and I cross the street to prepare for the daily activities. The day's work finishes and I am glad I made it. The next day brings the 'same old' again. It is a cycle, but it is meaningful for me and for what I want to accomplish.

Food business is time-consuming and requires lots of stamina. I choose to be a restaurateur. There is a saying: 'you make your bed, you lie in it', and I was prepared to do just that. I could not forget why I started in the first place.

As a teenager one of my favourite pastimes was playing the board game of checkers. It was intriguing and each time I played I learned something new. Winning called for tactfulness. I understood how to read the board layout in front of me. I knew when to pass in order to get the better advantage that would put me further ahead. My gut feeling would usually cause me to rethink a move. I sensed when it was perfect to jump. Don't be afraid to take that jump. Life wants you to take it.

When things were barely flourishing, I persisted despite the discomfort. In times like these, what you can do is live a life which says 'it is all right; this too shall pass'. Things do not stay the same. It can be difficult in the beginning, but tough times make you very alert. When everything seems to be going against you, do not lose sight of your original goal. Adopt optimistic behaviour. Each step taken in confidence is never lost, for it brings your reward. Nothing you have learnt is wasted.

Live a purposeful life. Nobody else can do it for you. The limitation that presents itself should not deter you. Find creative ways to make it happen. It has to be again and again. Follow your intuition.

No matter what comes to uproot us, no matter what arises, no matter the limits, we must find a way to make things work and be happy with the results.

In life you might think that you are all alone. You have been through so much that it is not always easy to talk about it. Know that other people also experience difficult times. We may not discuss them openly, but we more or less have quite a few things in common. We conquer many things; no one can know for us, but only ourselves. Life takes us on various and differing paths. There are many rivers to cross, but somehow we cross them and by grace we continue.

Life is a turnaround. After years of renting a commercial building I returned home with my business where I originally began. I am enjoying it and I am much happier. I have tried both ways, hence I can compare the two. If you want something big, then go for it, but I have come to the conclusion that keeping it simple makes me joyful. You know by your own experience.

Take your dream and bring it to actual existence. Build gradually; once you mean well there is no stopping you. Build towards something that gives you fulfillment. Build a legacy that inspires our future generations.

Establish a bond strong enough to withstand whatever the road ahead might bring. This life, especially now, calls for knowing who you are, what you are about and doing it. You need no one's permission. Do it with zeal and fervour. You can manifest whatever you imagine.

The employer and the employee

In the course Management of Human Resources I would have studied subjects related to the work place and discussed and analyzed case studies. I learnt about Herzberg's Motivation-Hygiene Theory and McGregor's Theory X and Theory Y. I was impressed with both. Maslow's Hierarchy of Needs, especially self-actualization, held my interest the most. I would have read about Peter Drucker, who invented the concept known as management by objectives and self-control. I was intrigued by Carl Jung.

I was ready to put these theories into practice, but I was in for an eye-opener. I noticed very early in the world of business that you have to deal accordingly and make adjustments to whatever you encounter. I realized I had to move beyond the theories. You cannot subject the operation of a business to mere theories. There is a difference between those theories and the real world of business. Direct experience is another ball game. I had to figure out the approach to take in relation to what was happening in the working environment at that particular moment. The case studies were theoretically based, but the practical was totally different.

Do these theories have a place in the workplace? Can I use them as a guideline?

In some ways these theories prepared me for the

business world. I could refer to them for guidelines and clarity and apply that knowledge when dealing with certain issues.

How do you motivate people? What makes them tick? Is it the physiological factors which are basically influenced by their needs? Could it be the psychological or something much deeper? It is not always easy to determine because a person's response or reaction is generally based on an internal ocurrence which is not easily seen.

Create an environment with harmony. Encourage others and have people around you who also encourage you and spur you on. The employee usually responds to friendly stimuli in the working environment and likewise the employer.

Tell the employees how much they are appreciated. This is likely to enhance the employees' attitude to work behaviour and satisfaction with their work. Reward them for contribution to the business. This can be done by enabling the employee to upgrade their qualifications by providing funds. In addition, the competency of the worker can be heightened with on-the-job training. These sessions help improve skills and oftentimes encourages creativity. This in-house practice shows the employee that you are interested in their welfare. Skills developed through continual training can benefit both employee and employer.

Are you highly motivated to achieve? What are the incentives? Is money only enough?

In the organization, you the owner have to demonstrate strength. Set high standards. Walk the talk. Action speaks louder than words. It earns you much admiration. Your uplifting Spirit puts people at ease and brings lightheartedness to the environment. Don't be too strait-laced. Relax the face muscles. Being too stiff or rigid can make you seem unapproachable, both to the employee as well as the customer. Be comfortable in your own skin. Have a pleasant, joyous disposition. It can be contagious. Note that honesty, sincerity and generosity are wholesome virtues that say much about your character.

Listening is good communication. You have to be able to hear what is not being said in the conversation. Read between the lines. Listening makes you more open. Take into consideration different ideas, views and opinions. Make sure the communication is clear with the other person. Be regardful and observant.

Can the employee be the owner's friend? Can the owner be the employee's confidante? Friendship develops when people feel welcome and at ease in your company. The individual becomes closer to the person who cares, shows love and respect, and proves to be confidential. There is still that bond even after many years although both have gone their separate ways.

Today I am delighted to say some of my former employees are now budding entrepreneurs in the food industry.

Times are changing. In fact, life is ever changing. Things do not remain the same. For instance, historically men were only considered for certain work. Now women are doing jobs previously thought to be only for men and vice versa. Females in various cultures had expected roles in the society, whereas males were expected to be in the frontline. Today you have several female business owners. The cultural values of the socio-economic structure have changed tremendously and we find ourselves shifting and evolving in order to maintain stability.

The soul of a business

Every organization has a 'soul', therefore you must guard your soul. Why am I talking about the soul of a business? Because I have recognized and identified with it. I have experienced it in my own business.

The growth of the soul should have positive energy to take it to the highest level—good thoughts, good vibes, good understanding to uplift it. You must know when to eliminate negativity from the business before it hinders its development. You have to check constantly before it chokes your crop.

The soul is sacred. It is woven with love. It is crafted to succeed. There is no mistake, for in itself the soul is a masterpiece, a unique creation designed with Divine care and protection. A well-balanced soul is able to accommodate goodness and give out goodness.

The demand is great and the supply is limitless. This light would be the love of light. A light to feed the world not only for the physical but also mental, spiritual and emotional. The universe embraces the soul.

How I did it

With over 25 years of running a restaurant I have gathered many insights and I am extremely delighted to share them. The experiences led me to write this book. To be able to document all that I have discovered would require more than one book. Each day I am filled with more knowledge and my experience grows. I will be forever writing.

In my studies in Hotel Management and Institutional Catering I was taught the major aspects involved in the operation of a business. I applied this knowledge for managing the restaurant. What you learn never leaves you. It has in the long run proven to be a good investment. It has served me well.

Basic common sense is always at the forefront when managing a business. Basic common sense helps you to run a successful business and to stay in business.

Every day I told myself I have come too far from where I started to give up. I didn't know where it was going to take me, but somehow deep within I was compelled to continue doing whatever was needed. Now I can say it led me to writing about life in business.

Don't get me wrong, sometimes you may have to walk away. Everyone's situation is different. Do what is in your best interest. You can release a thing without giving up on yourself. You might be saving yourself from something further down the road. When you have done everything possible, put down the heavy load you are carrying. Somehow you know when enough is enough. It is usually that moment when you say 'I can do better'.

You might have made projections on where you want to be at a certain time. Know your capabilities. You may have cash flow projections for a specific period, whether weekly or monthly, but incoming money from sales are below your expenditure. Don't despair. I grew up hearing this saying: "don't lie down and play dead". Get up and stand firm. Keep on. Have a healthy outlook on life until things get better. Let your mischance be the opportunity for a new path. You have a lot to live for.

I continue to learn and grow. Every day I am learning something new.

We should learn to master the art of continuing without being distracted. Yes, temptations come our way, but as long as we keep focused everything falls into place. We can do it with guidance and love.

I ask myself many questions. Some I can answer, others I leave alone. Nonetheless, when I can't place a 'finger' on whatever is happening in my life or the business, I can still say that God is good to me. Each day when I am faced with the tasks at hand I remain steadfast to my vision. Life, with all its different explorations, is waiting to be discovered.

Be fearless when the unfamiliar shows up.

Remain undisturbed. The answer is often there staring us straight in the face, but the pressures of life prevent us from seeing.

What is life to you? Mankind is always searching; we search until we find. Find your own path and follow it. Own your story.

I have discovered a lot from having a business. Business is more than a means of providing an income for basic necessities and for everyday living. It is years of learning with unsureness, disappointments, mishaps, pressures and emotions, yet full of passion and love for the things I am doing. I have learnt to live through the trials; to persevere and to prevail. In the process I have discovered much about my higher self. It takes you through valleys, but the beauty of it is that you bloom and advance to better things. Some days I had an overflowing joy for no reason. I am conscious of the Divine presence that stayed with me throughout the years.

Whatever is, is fine; for the knowledge I have accumulated over the years serves me well.

Things shifted. I would not give up, for I was determined to make it. Passion took me through tough times. I could not stand still; I was compelled to go forward. I found my strength and used it categorically to make my dreams happen. Life has taken me through many routes, yet I live. Yet I persevere. I keep going on, not even knowing sometimes what for.

You plant and it grows of its own accord.

Life is really a cycle

It is amazing how things can come full circle. Before I had officially established the restaurant, I started from home. Now I am back home with the business and it feels good. In most instances in life, home is the place we usually return to. It is a safe haven for comfort when we need it.

After years of renting a commercial building, I assessed what was happening and was not pleased. More money was going out than was coming in. I knew I had to keep costs down. Suddenly it dawned on me that renting a building was unnecessary. I could easily work from home. Further assessments led to clear-cut action. I decided to move the business home, as there was enough space to accommodate it. Some renovations were required to make it functional, but nothing too major.

There are advantages to this move. There is natural lighting and ventilation, hence no need for air-conditioning units or having lights on all day. Paying a mortgage, rent for the building and utility bills, it made sense to have everything under one roof, thus reducing the overheads. The expenses were drastically cut, bringing a feeling of exoneration.

Furthermore, my home is situated a mere stone's throw away from the previous business site. I no longer have to cross the street early in the mornings and this is a breath of fresh air. The home-based location can handle what I am doing. The size of the business is perfect. I am at liberty to do any remodeling to the property as I see fit.

I knew it was time to shift and time for restructuring. I knew it was time for action to reduce overheads. I followed my own heart, and by doing just that I have recovered that drive to put energy into my work. I can truly say that was one of the best decisions I have ever made in my life. Today more people are working from their homes.

Lesson

Your expenditure cannot be more than your sales. Make a firm decision and honestly live with it.

There was genuine support during the whole journey. Somehow when I needed help, it turned up and assisted me. At times like these I felt the Creator's nearness strongly. I kept going and going, nursing and feeding the dream until it bore fruit.

In business, know what matters. It is your guide. No-one said it was easy, but you got the door open. Look back at where you have come from. The contribution that you make is worthwhile.

As you keep going forward, the closer you are to your victory. Whether it is a new chapter or a new page, know that you are forever guided. You eventually win.

Happy Memories: The Current Years

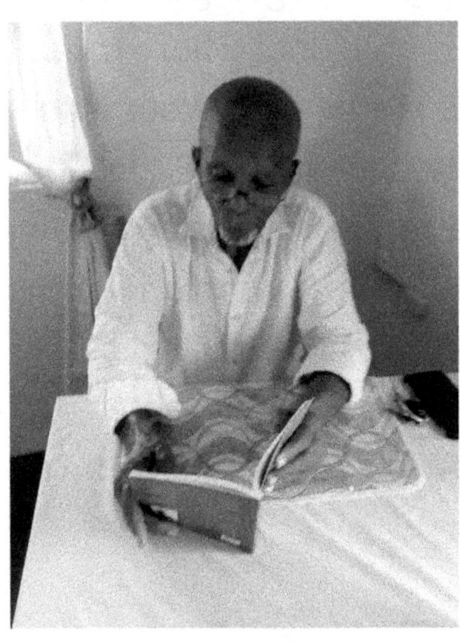

Denis McIntosh, a loyal client, perusing the book *You Can Breathe.*

Wilma Halloway. She still frequents the restaurant after many years.

Arturo Tappin, who is a strong supporter of Vegan Cottage.

Roger Moore. *We know where to find you at lunch time.*

David and Melanie from Canada.

Shinobeau, a Japanese vegan chef and teacher.

Uncle Kelvin (right) with his family from England.

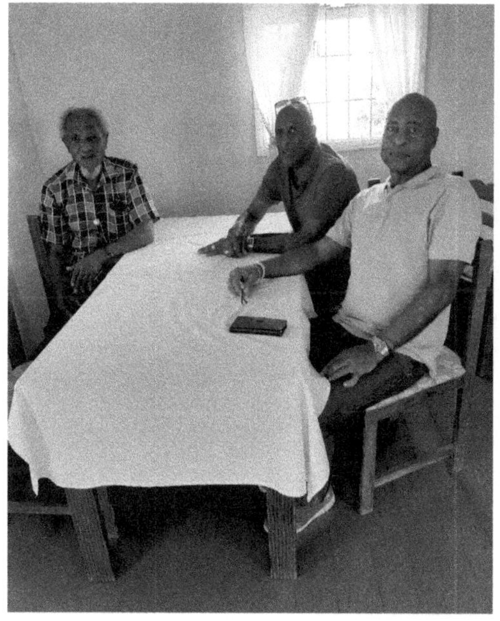

Ricky Hinds (right) who has been a repeat customer, took time out to relax with his friends Timmy and Kelvin.

Deepu Panjwani (left) and Michael Thorpe (right). They are business owners and were staunch clients for numerous years.

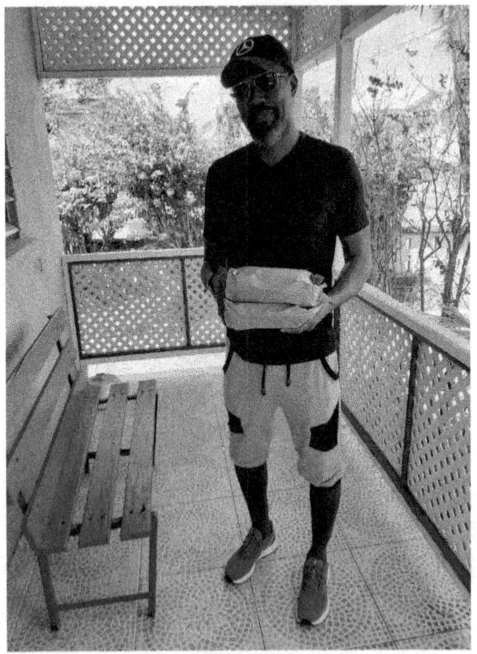

Shawn Adams, a faithful client who lives in my neighbourhood.

Ermine Barker from London. She comes often to have lunch with us whenever she is in Barbados.

Bliss Cadogan, from England, always come to Vegan Cottage when she is on holiday.

Ian Durant is a valued client and the restaurant is blessed to have had someone like him all through these years.

It's Sade's birthday (in the floral dress), and Jamila, Shomari and Terry are having a special get-together with her for the occasion.

In loving memory of the late Harold Hoyte. Harold was truly an outstanding client and treasured friend. I will never forget his enlightening talks and his moral support.

A Grateful Heart

People often ask me what is my secret. Gratitude is my secret. I give gratitude in advance. I start my day and end my day with giving thanks. I find that to be grateful brings a calmness and joy within. Things are not always the way we want them to be. But what really matters is what we are doing at that particular moment. Whatsoever I am doing, gratitude is present.

Value what you have. Appreciate and enjoy your blessings. Be thankful for the beautiful people in your life. Be thankful for the wonders that occur day by day. Be thankful for the beauty in flowers, plants, birds, rainbows, the sunrise and sunset, and experience the higher power at work.

I have experienced kindness from my clients. I am delighted to be associated with them. It is a wonderful feeling. It was the encouragement from the clients that also kept me going all these years. I felt the sincerity of their patronage. There are loyal clients who still keep my stove burning. I am grateful. Loyalty is very important in a person's life. Many of my clients go back to the inception of the business. There were many days I enjoyed talking to my clients and having a hearty laugh. Laughter is the best medicine. It is a pleasure to interact with people, whether it is sharing ideas or having a good, joyful conservation. For all of this I am grateful.

I am thankful for the opportunity to have my dreams fulfilled. At this moment I am thankful for the insight to write this book. I give thanks for my being and my existence. I love life and for this I am so grateful. What are you grateful for?

Love is God
Love brings goodness
God is in the goodness

I stop for a moment, look around me and I am conscious of how much I give the Creator thanks for. I am conscious of the goodness in my life. I acknowledge how divine order works for me. Goodness and love continue to follow me.

Times I felt peace

The simple things in life perk up the day. Live a simple life.

I stood beside the protective rail looking at the ocean around me. The clear water looked enticing. As the waves broke I could smell the saltiness from the sea. I watched how the crabs move swiftly along the sand. Yachts and smaller boats were further out in the ocean. The golden sunset over the horizon was a sight to be admired. This was my escape. I felt peace.

The drive was unforgettable. I enjoyed every aspect of it. I wandered to a remote area overlooking vast land. The view was magnificent. The mile trees were a definite landmark. Houses were scattered in the distance. The atmosphere of pure tranquility was appealing. It was cool and refreshing. There was such blissfulness amidst the whole setting and I drifted off in meditation. I gave myself quiet thoughts. Each thought was a prayer. I felt peace.

I woke early, as usual. I was in the kitchen preparing the day's menu. I glanced up at the window and saw a full moon in all its splendour. I pulled back the curtain to get a better view. I was in awe at the radiant glow. I felt peace instantly.

I withdrew myself from all the activities going on and went outside for a while. I looked at the birds, the trees, the flowering plants, the blue sky and the fluffy white clouds. Observing the beauty of nature somehow revitalized my Spirit. I felt peace.

It is not costly to surround yourself with beauty or to inhale the sweet fragrance of the flowers or to enjoy nature's beauty.

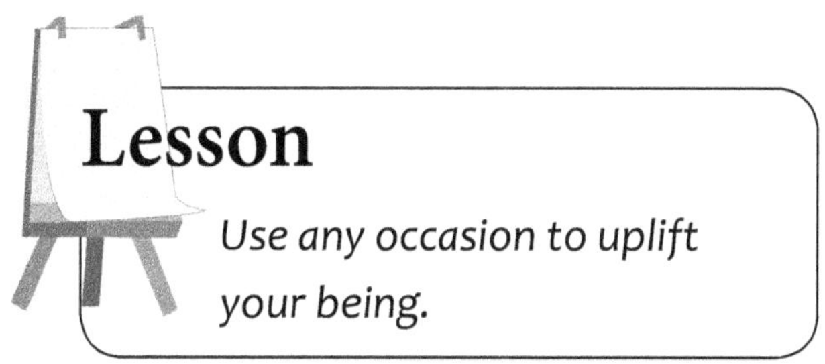

Lesson

Use any occasion to uplift your being.

The guiding light

At some point in time you get tired. I get tired too, but although I am tired the dream would not let me give up. There is this force within that will not leave me alone. It keeps pushing me and somehow my energy recharges and there is a deep desire to perform at my best. It's so mystical. It is indescribable.

The Creator is with me every step of the way. I focus on the good instead of negativity, and bless my works and financial gains continually. Being financially independent helps you to be free.

I go within to the God of benevolence when I am overwhelmed. It is that place where I am trusting myself no matter what happens until I can see the fruits of my labour.

The strength that gave me encouragement to continue is at its peak. The Most High led me and guided my footsteps all the way and I am happy. *Oh Creator, my friend, my comforter and provider I am filled with gratitude for grace and love. I did not throw in the towel. You have directed me along the right path and I kept on.*

Traveling this road brought some discomfort but I held on, knowing whatever it was would once and for all be finally broken. Now it is wonderful and great days are with me. The emotional energy is your cover.

Amidst the trials I kept on for I knew the source of my supply and abundance. My energy came from the source. Why then did I have misfortunes? To show me my further potential and capabilities. My tests were challenging, yet I had to pass them with honours. I would not fold up. My trials have made me stronger. Every trial is a lesson. Learn from the lesson.

As you navigate through life, the credentials are patience, courage and will power. In addition zeal, endurance, discipline and perseverance. Know your true inner self. Know your purpose, your full potential, and appreciate goodness.

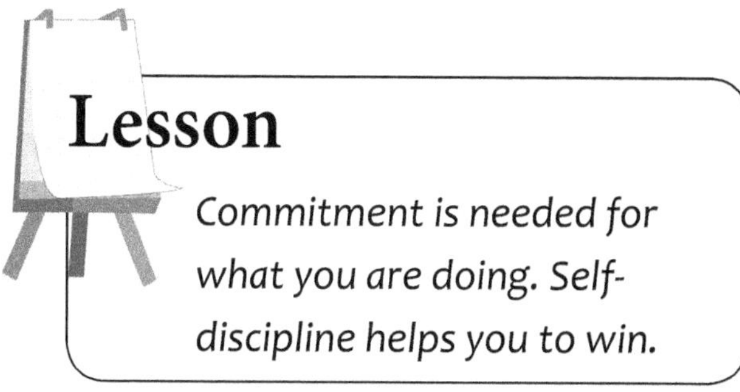

Persistence and determination won at the really testing times. When things got tough, I held on, for it was just before the dawn and I could detect light in the sky. The sun came out and shone in my life.

Fill me with your Divine love until I am lifted higher and higher. Let my mind be quiet so I can hear and interpret the voice.

Higher state of consciousness

It is no longer a dream; it is part of you and you continue to feed it. We have a power ingrained in us to make it happen. You know what you want to accomplish. You can smell it .You can see it. Trust what you see with your inner eye. You can taste it. Once you taste it, you are hungry to make it happen. Feel it, touch it. It is within your reach. Others may not understand what is driving you, but for some reason you know it is achievable. Stand by your mission until it blossoms.

Align yourself to a higher vibration. Flourish spiritually. Flourish financially. There is that innate ability to call forth what you need. Take your power back. Accept that power within, a power rich and full of love, and show up for yourself.

Avow the connection. The realization and enlightenment are amazing. The spiritual connection to higher consciousness is undeniable. You know when you are connected to the source. Words are limited to describe it. It is your experience and sometimes it cannot be expressed.

When you relax it comes. Be dauntless. Have unwavering trust. Trust divine intelligence. There is no limit to the things you can achieve in your life.

Prayer

During the period from 1996 to 2021 I had written several prayers. Most of them were centered towards giving thanks. Prayer was my shield. Prayer gave me inner comfort. Prayer helps me to unlock the truth. Prayer was my fire, my warmth and my strength. I wrote how I was feeling. Each prayer changed according to what was happening in my life. Whether it is business or life, you have to identify with that outlet that brings some kind of calmness. Your own heart already knows. Many days I have seen the fullness of God's love. God is what you want God to be. God is who you want God to be.

Prayer is a part of my everyday life and living. It is invaluable. Why do I pray? Prayer is that conversation I have with my inner self to get me through most things. It brings guidance to make the right decisions. It brings further patience. Prayer allowed me to handle the tough days. Prayer was an avenue to help me to cope. Prayer calmed me. It brought an assurance and there was that sense of knowing it is going to be fine.

Prayer has power. I can attest to this about prayer through my own experiences. When I pray I draw to myself fresh energy so strong that I get up and start moving. I no longer feel like stopping. Prayer is what I am experiencing deep within my being. Prayer keeps me grounded. It allows me to move forward with more confidence in the good times and the not so good times.

Prayer is holistic. Prayer gives me a sweet peace. It brings an inner richness. Prayer brings grace and grace is joy. Whatever you do with joy is a prayer.

Compilation of my selected prayers

Oh sweet provider of the universe enlighten me with your goodness, that I may forever know you care while searching and waiting, but in all patience knowing that you always provide. I get it when I need it. It can be immediate or slightly delayed, nevertheless I get it. Replenish my soul. My praise is to the Creator and nourisher of life. Guide me in your light. Protect and guard over my life. Oh bless me.

***

I am here because a way was made and I travelled in that light. Divine Love directs and guides my path. I made it through with grace.

I am connected to the source of abundance. Your Divine presence dwells within me. I acknowledge it daily in my life.

***

When I thought things were not working out for me, now I know that I was being shifted so

I could move forward to greater things. You have carried me when I had little strength to a secure place. The waters were murky, rough; the business needed you as the commander. You took over and brought it to safety. You quieted the disturbance and brought it to calm waters. I am at peace.

You have sustained me and guided me in all my business affairs. God's love is rare. I held on to the business knowing that Divine presence was with me. Even in the darkest night I saw your light and I knew you were by my side.

The lightning flashes. The thunder roars. The rain pours down. The piercing wind howls. I cry out with my whole heart. Mother earth hears and cries with me. My soul is at peace.

I am forever guided to my daily bread. This 'bread' is my sustenance. It fills me and brings inner joy for physical, emotional, mental and spiritual needs. I feel much contentment. Glory be to the Creator within who has raised my consciousness that I can acknowledge my higher self. I relax knowing we are one in this journey called life.

My meditation and my prayers have touched a lighted source. I feel joy in the morning. Let me submerge in it to the full extent possible in this life. Oh guide and protect me. I am your child. Lift me up higher.

Let me give thanks for allowing me to keep going even when I did not know how I would get it done. Let me give thanks for giving me the strength and boldness each day to carry on and to complete. Let me give thanks for being my spiritual guide. Let me give thanks for guiding me to the literature which gave me motivation and inspiration. The encouragement to continue no matter what comes my way. Thanks for listening and hearing when I call. Thanks for your care, for being my friend. Thanks for the things which brought me to greater realization. In my self-exploration I have discovered that it was all meant to be. Thanks for the things that brought spiritual enrichment. Thanks for the things which have brought true meaning and a new perspective for living.

Thanks for the Divine energy that took over when the stumbling blocks were too many.

I am overflowing with a burst of energy. My higher self knew that I could not run away. I held on to life knowing my Creator was with me. I am in awe with your wonders and cherish our close relationship.

Everything on this earth is for us to enjoy; let us see it in that light. To see how far we have come. To see the beauty in the flowers, plants, birds, the double rainbow, the sunrise and sunset, in people's faces.

The Supreme is my light. Success comes, for you want me to do well in every area of my life. I feel your presence in all my works and living. Love grows and fulfills my very being; that ecstasy is reached to its highest. Negative external forces cannot penetrate my heart, for I have a thick wall of love to shut them out. My soul is lifted higher.

I have felt much anxiety, yet my life has been preserved. I go within to the God of peace. I find calmness/equanimity there. My wearied bones are brought to life. I am overjoyed. Contentment has come over my soul. Oh Magnificent One, you are worthy of my praise. Let my life be forever enriched with your wonders, your grace, your favour, your love, your kindness, your care, your guidance, your provision. It is truly amazing.

In my meditation the realization and enlightenment are divine. My courage and strength allow me to conquer. The source of my supply and abundance are sure.

Oh Creator, my invincible, your works are stupendous. I acknowledge your wisdom, understanding and good counsel. My soul give thanks to your name. I am filled with the joy of your closeness.

Oh Creator, lead me with the power of determination that I would not surrender under any pressure. Uplift my soul, my being that I would not be disheartened when I come to a standstill. Show me your unconditional love as I continue this journey. Let me drink the pure water from your fountain. Let me bear fruitage of happiness and command peace to my very being. Take me to that higher place where we are joined together as one—the revelation of oneness. Be my lighthouse so that I can see my ships coming in.

The presence of the Creator is with me. You are my sweetest joy. I am sustained by the Divine consciousness which kept me going every day. I have a roof over my head, food on my table and love in my heart. I cannot complain, for the beauty of life surrounds me. Thanks is forever on my lips for all I have received.

I found God everywhere and in everything. In my situations, experiences, my heart, my emotions, my thoughts, in nature, in people. Whatever I do God Consciousness is present.

God is in my meditation. In meditation my body is recharged, the energy flows, ideas come and creativity improves.

I arise and give thanks. The Supreme Creator is my companion, travelling with me all the way.

Thanks for your companionship along those long, lonely roads when my body became weary. You guided my steps and comforted my mind with sweet whispers.

I cannot deny you for your presence is constant in my life. I felt your infinite power as you renewed me day after day. You always deliver and every experience took me to a higher level of knowing you more and more. There is an inner cry which opens up the lungs of my very existence, connecting me to that universal energy. There is such momentum that my work becomes soul-satisfying.

The fire rushed towards me, I saw the fury flames. I felt the heat, then the stinging pain, but somehow I was shielded and I was spared. My protector was on duty. This is why I give thanks and praise. I have been fed and nourished in my time of need. My provider was on duty. This is why I give thanks and praises. I have managed and risen amidst the pressure and adversity. My comforter was on duty. This is why I give thanks and praises.

I looked in the mirror
Love stared me in the face
A sweet love; a pure love
My life has been preserved.
I exhale and inhale deeply.
Let me enjoy beauty and peace
You are my comforter,
I saw you in the darkness.

I saw you in the light.
I embrace your precious love.

Increase the flow of humility. You give me the enthusiasm to continue. I can see the works of your hands in the business; I thank you for your guidance and love.

Give thanks in glory, thanks in praise, thanks in song, thanks in prayers and thanks in my daily works. Thanks to the Creator who cared and lifted me from turbulent waters. God provided the calm.

God has brought a freshness to my being.
God has brought sweetness to my life.
God has brought an inner light.

Thanks for providing for my every need. I cried with much appreciation for the gifts. For the genuine support. Oh, it is a pleasure to be in contact with the highest, the Supreme majesty in holy splendour. There is an inner calmness to my being.

My weary body is revived. At the real testing times I felt love within my heart. When I was alone you were my invisible friend and I value your sacredness.

My enthusiasm and passion about life engulf me. It is inspiring and is way beyond all I could ever dream of that there is a burning desire to be highly productive.

It is the 'trust' which allows me to know it will happen no matter what. I find something to celebrate. There is a true meaning and a new perspective for living.

I found satiety in my food and drink. A drink so refreshing that I forever want to drink. A food rich in divine love that it brings satisfaction.

The troubled waters have ceased
The dark clouds have been removed.
Move into radiance and forever shine.
Forget sorrows, forget pain
Rise upon your light and love
Rise in your own consciousness.

The words of my prayer awaken my heart, my soul. I am uplifted and I feel the revival in Spirit.

Divine support fuels my inner strength. Glory be to the highest. Without that Divine presence I might have buckled when I was faced with misfortunes. I am not ashamed of the Creator who knows my name and has provided for me over many years. I have realized God through my sorrows and through love. God is my buttress.

Nourisher of life I give you thanks. I see beauty in your love. Sustainer of life I give you thanks. In every breath, in every moment I am conscious of your presence. Thanks for keeping me and allowing me to put things together despite the situations I found myself in. At times I could not comprehend the process, but it has opened my mind to greater understanding. I was shown the way and directed to a clearer path when I was unsure. I opened up my inner being to love, power, goodness, grace, favour and blessings. I am thankful for the kindness and generosity expressed towards me.

In the still of the night.
Speak joy to my soul
Speak love to my heart
That I may feel your warm embrace

Oh bless your works continually. Fulfill your purpose on this earth. You have power to win, to be victorious. Who else but you can provide it? What is damaged can be repaired.

What is closed can be opened. What is broken can be fixed. Who is better to take care of the business but the owner? You have its welfare at heart.

Mankind in his essence.
Mankind in his glory.
What more can we do?

***

THE INSPIRING HEART

The nature of contentment fills my life with merriment. I have all I need at this present moment. My cup overflows. Daily I give thanks, gratitude is forever. My enthusiasm and passion about life comes from deep within. It is inspiring. My passion and gratitude become prayerfulness. I allow it to shine forth in my daily life.

My heart is saturated with love. It touches every part of my being. There is that tingling excitement. The awakened energy brings freshness. My heart is full with delight. Oh Creator as I meditate, my heart is open to your very goodness. Whisper in my ears.

*Whisper all the things you want me to know.
It is our secret dialogue. Gratitude pours from
my heart and it brings bliss and reverence.*

God is love
Love guides
Love teaches
Love preserves
Love nourishes
Love sustains
Love protects
Love embraces
Love comforts
Love provides
Love is enough.

Far from Finished

It was December 29th 1996 when the restaurant was officially opened, and I am still here with the business. I have reached my silver jubilee as a restaurateur, and I am exhilarated.

Throughout this book I have looked primarily at challenges, obstacles and difficulties—things that may throw us off. However, they are an integral part of the growth process. At times our lives might seem complex, but we should keep doing. We are capable of doing the impossible. I know it can be done because I have done it myself.

Many entrepreneurs would tell you that we did what was necessary to make it work until the breakthrough came. No matter how severe the storm, how dark the night, how bumpy the road or high the mountain, our survival instinct kicked in and got us through. We learned how to continue in spite of setbacks and found ways to be sustainable. The most beautiful thing is that we grew where we were planted.

Are you living up to your highest potential? What is your reason for getting up in the morning?

What inspires you? Sometimes the script is already written. Are you the main star? Are you the supporting actress or actor? Whatever role you play, bring your personal touch to it and radiate the pure light from within.

Every chapter of life's journey can be mesmerizing. Each page wants you to turn to the next and the next. The story is spellbinding and has you in suspense, not exposing much, but you have an inkling of how it is going to unravel. What you have predicted occurs. Contrariwise, there can be a twist in the story and what you never thought of took place. Nevertheless something special usually materializes when you didn't expected it to happen.

My journey is far from finished. What I have come to know is that the unwillingness to quit has taken me further ahead. I have also come to know that the mystical events which transpired in my life have opened up other avenues for me. There were times I felt so inspired that I prayed earnestly. My prayers were not to ask for anything, but to align with my dream and see it manifest. It goes beyond faith; it is an inner knowing, magnified with Divine will.

Personal growth

It was tough, but too many years were invested to become wearisome. I am still figuring things out, but I follow my own map. I now work alone and I am comfortable with that. Sometimes you have to continue the journey alone in order to carry on your vision. Being a sole proprietor, I am the 'chief cook and bottle washer'. I function in every area of the business, but after doing this work for such a long time it has become naturally effortless. It is like breathing.

Working solo from home is convenient in many ways. I love my space. I am operating on a smaller scale, but I am satisfied. I have more freedom to do the things I like than when I started the restaurant. I function at my own pace. I just do what is necessary. I act out of spontaneity. I work much easier and smarter and simpler. There is no expectation. There is liberation. I call that growth.

I can remember the times when I got up before three o'clock in the morning and when I worked seven days a week. I was the first one in and the last one out. Now I work fewer hours and I grant myself days off. I have learnt that after many years of substantial work, by working less I am able to do other meaningful things with my life such as writing this book, which I find to be gratifying.

We have been conditioned to think that in order to be successful we must work really hard, but I differ from that way of thinking. I must admit that in the early stages of the business I worked arduously. However, there are practical ways to work smarter rather than harder, and get the task done. Over time you get it right.

The load has lightened and there is so much ease on my body. I no longer rush or hurry and I am enjoying it. I am more sensible in my approach to most things because of various lessons. They have brought me to a place where whatever seems to be happening around me, I embrace and savour the present moment. I acknowledge infinite blessings.

I never knew that business would lead me to such profound things. The practical experience is immeasurable.

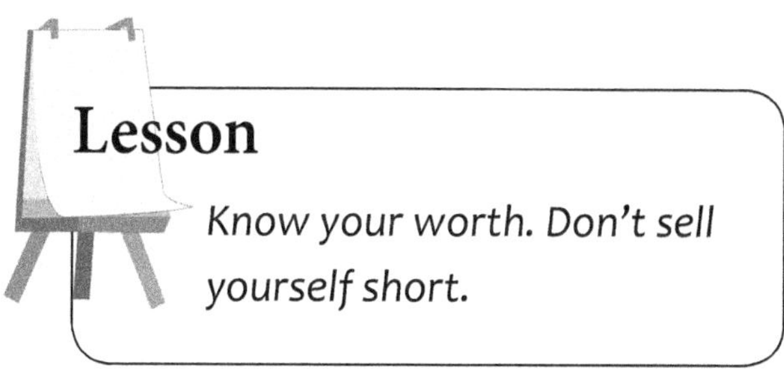

Lesson

Know your worth. Don't sell yourself short.

The pursuit of purpose

I wrote about taking risks in an earlier chapter. I didn't have collateral, but I had much to share. My vision was vast and that is what overshadowed the financial concerns. I even made a pie chart wheel and divided the circle into slices. Each slice represented what I wanted to accomplish.

You may think that money is the answer to most of the things you want to achieve in your life, but it is only part of the whole process. Don't spend your time and energy living on the edge. Start with what you have at your disposal. I have come to a place in my life where I do not give power to what I do not have, but instead I give power to what I have. Every day I write the things I am grateful for in my journal.

Encourage yourself as you walk your path. The one you are looking for, is you. You are your wisest teacher. Be satisfied with the work you have already done and as you advance, make things easier for yourself. Value your life. Who else is going to?

As human beings we face incredible lessons. I have received what the lessons taught me and I thank them. Regard life as a terrific school. If the unthinkable happens, you have to rise above it.

Deal with any underlying issues in a clear-headed manner. Keep on traveling and show acts of courage. Speak boldly to your desires. Don't limit yourself. Open the gem lying within and discover your greater self.

Does anything have an end? In my experience I have come to realize that every end is a new beginning. That's life.

As you pursue your purpose, have some fun and enjoy your moments. It is good for your wellness. Improvement of self also comes with leisure. Dance and sing some more. Don't be too serious. Don't let life pass you by. Celebrate life. The universe will rejoice with you.

Sometimes I would stop in my busy-ness and take in the surroundings. I notice that overnight the flower buds have opened up, revealing their inner beauty. I gaze at the trail of ants moving slowly across the driveway, probably in search of food. There is much wisdom in observing them.

Sometimes I would reminisce about those fantastic events I catered for during the business years. I can never forget that first wedding and the exquisite garden where it was held. The sumptuous vegan dishes and my friend Pauline's mouthwatering Paw-paw Crumble which complemented the other desserts. The moonlight had an enchanting effect on the whole setting and the romantic music was perfect for the occasion.

Simplify your life and be cheerful. Always be thankful for another day.

As an entrepreneur I embrace the multifaceted life and I have found it to be an asset. It has sharpened my wit and I am self-motivated to get things done. I push myself beyond the comfort zone. Sometimes we risk the known for the unknown, and it leads us to infinite possibilities.

As we pursue our purpose there will be tears, pain, joy, sorrow, sadness and happiness. They give us our own story. We must acknowledge that sadness and sorrow are not permanent. They are powerful experiences in our lives and guide us to our innermost wisdom. The tears and the pain are the opening of the way for heightened awareness. The joy and the happiness are surges of emotions which connect us to peace. Peace is power.

As we pursue our purpose, we are curious about how the race will finish. However, we must first step over each hurdle carefully. Needless to say, it is human nature to always seek answers. There is a hunger to know, but the truth is often revealed in the course of time. In the meanwhile, quiet the mind and just listen. Look within yourself and discover your wonderful existence.

There was a time I took three months leave from the business. During that period I was well rested, but I felt something was missing. I somehow knew that unless I brought my work to its full growth, I would not be complete. The magnetic pull was strong and I was ready to get back to it. When I returned to the restaurant, my clients greeted me with lots of hugs and bright smiles. From those loving gestures, I clearly understood what the universe was telling me and my thirst for action was intensified. I dig deeper to carry on the mantle. The universe gives us clues and it is for us to recognize them, lest we miss the opportunity for moving forward.

Who are we really? What is our cosmic purpose?

Everything is connected in some way. Our behaviour influences our families and our friends. Our behaviour impacts on our neighbourhood, the wider community and the world. Our sustainable habits help our planet. We are as strong as our strongest link.

Look back at your life and you will recall those people who gave support at crucial stages. We are forever taken care of, and our needs are constantly being supplied. Simply love. It provides nourishment for the soul. As we interact with each other more favourably, there is that beauty within that we cannot withhold. In our giving, we receive more.

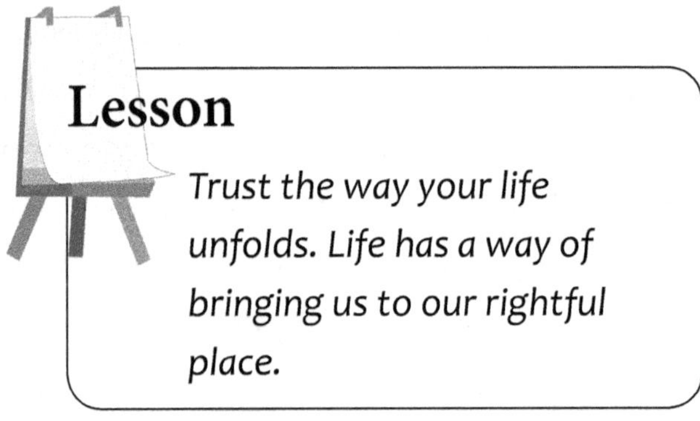

Lesson

Trust the way your life unfolds. Life has a way of bringing us to our rightful place.

The journey continues

I have my aspirations. I know where I started from. When you have witnessed so much nothing can beat those experiences as they expand your consciousness. Life becomes even more meaningful. Every day is wonderful as you follow your heart.

The big question is, would I do it all over again? The answer is twofold. Sometimes I would say yes, and other times I say no. It depends on how I am looking at it. I am not sure, but I have no regrets. I got to meet the most amazing, remarkable people.

Furthermore, I have made friendships with local, regional and international clients whom I might not have come into contact with had it not been for the restaurant business. I have made my contribution to humanity and I am ecstatic about that. There is a richness in service.

The journey has begun to excite me more and more. I am enjoying the process, looking forward for the next phase not knowing what is in store for me. I am comfortable with not knowing. There is a new fire and I am eager to get on. I am more determined to walk my path. I look at my life, what I have been through, how far I have come, and my Spirit rises. Deep within I know I will continue until it has finished teaching me.

Key Points

- Mankind is resilient.
- Raise your energy level through harmonious thoughts.
- Open your mind to rich ideas. There is always a surplus.
- Be confident and let your light flow continuously.
- Friendship is a priceless gift.
- Deposit love; withdraw love.
- Celebrate your being. Choose to be happy.
- Never forget that others helped and appreciate their generosity.
- Use your Imagination to create your own world.
- When we are in alignment with our vision it will manifest.
- Be your own creator. Use the creativity you possess.
- Embrace life at every moment. We are responsible for ourselves.
- We learn from things all around us. They help us to grow.
- Remember that when you use what you have

on hand, it will meet your needs.

- Life insists on change for its expansion. You have everything to gain through the change.
- People generally perform better when they are in a nurturing environment.
- Prioritize your time and say no to unimportant things.
- Find meaning in the hard moments and in the joyous moments.
- Regardless of opposing circumstances, you should dream big.
- Finish each day and be contented.
- Laughter is the best medicine.
- Learn from your mistake and be done with it.
- Pause in the middle of your busy day. It helps quiet the mind.
- Be thankful for the things we have already in our lives.
- Be thankful that your financial obligations were met.
- Be thankful for divine fulfillment in your personal affairs.
- Be thankful for divine restoration in your mind, body and soul.
- We all have something to offer. Light up the world with your light.

About the Author

photo by Reco Moore

Augustina Hinds has been a restaurateur for over twenty-five years. She is qualified in Hotel Management and Institutional Catering, Food Science Technology, Holistic Nutrition and other related disciplines. She has gained experience in teaching, participating in healthy lifestyles seminars, exhibitions and promotional events. Augustina is an award-winning Culinary Artist. She is also the author of *You Can Breathe* and *Vegan Conscious: A journey to Sustainable Health and Wellness.*

Other books by Augustina Hinds: